ENTREPRENEUR'S GUIDE TO

THE LEAN BRAND™

ENTREPRENEUR'S GUIDE TO

THE LEAN BRAND™

HOW BRAND INNOVATION TRANSFORMS ORGANIZATIONS, DISCOVERS NEW VALUE AND CREATES PASSIONATE CUSTOMERS

JEREMIAH GARDNER
WITH BRANT COOPER

ILLUSTRATIONS BY @FAKEGRIMLOCK

ENTREPRENEUR'S GUIDE TO THE LEAN BRAND

HOW BRAND INNOVATION TRANSFORMS ORGANIZATIONS,
DISCOVERS NEW VALUE AND CREATES PASSIONATE CUSTOMERS

Copyright © 2014 by Jeremiah Gardner

Published by Market By Numbers, LLC, San Diego, California

SERIES EDITOR:	PRODUCTION EDITOR:	ILLUSTRATIONS BY:
Brant Cooper	Eric Nelson	@FAKEGRIMLOCK

BOOK DESIGNER:	JOIN THE WORLDWIDE COMMUNITY:
Jeremiah Gardner and 1106 Design	http://leanbrandbook.com

ISBN-13: 978-0-9961007-2-4

Printed and bound in the United States of America.

For My One, Till The End of Our Days . . .

A SPECIAL THANKS

The truth about the development, writing, and publishing of *The Lean Brand* comes down to a single word—*community*. It was a *community* that brought this book to life. A *community* that has rallied around a new way of thinking. And a *community* that has shed light on a new path for brand innovation. Without the *Lean Brand Community*, who believed in this project enough to pre-order a book when it was merely a crowdpublishing campaign, we may have never got through the ups and downs of publishing this book. Your feedback, support, enthusiasm, and grace have brought new meaning to the word community.

Thank you for being a part of this community,

Jeremiah & Brant

The Lean Brand EARLY ADOPTERS:

Aamplify

Aaron Matys

Alan Turner

Alexa Roman

Alison Anthoine

Aliza "The Great" Stein

Amber De Barge and Catalina Kesler

Andy Fleming

Annette Mason

Ben Metcalf

Ben Spear

Brady Brim-DeForest

Brendon Livingstone

Bridget Ayers

Bryan Hall

Carrie Layne

Charmane H. Sellers

ChefsRoll.com

Collin Graves

Dan Keldsen

Dan Raine

Daniel James Scott

David C. Cohen

David Telleen-Lawton

David Welch

Deane Sloan

Debbie Wooldridge	Nik Souris
Dee Copeland Patience	Noble Digital
Digital-Telepathy	Nordkapp, Helsinki
Donovan Keme	Oinkodomeo
Emiliano Villarreal	Paul Clifford
Gerhard Müller	Phelan Riessen
Giuseppe Costabile	philosophie
Guy Vincent	Preston Bates
Ivan Rapin-Smith	Rachel Colic
James Kern	Ralf Westbrock
James Wallace	Randy Apuzzo
Jason SurfrApp	Randy Hunt
JC "The Envisioneer" Otero	Raomal Perera
Jeff 'SKI' Kinsey	Robert Yard
Jessica Howell	Roberto Magnifico
Jessie Gardner	Ron Quartel
Joe Messina	Ruben Cantu
Jon Fauver	Sachin Pawaskar
Juan-Carlos Otero	Scott Bales
Karsten Gresch	Scott Gillespie
Lisa Plener	Scott Zimmer
Laurence McCahill	Simon Stehle
Marco Esteban Calzolari	Spike Morelli
Marketing Stream	Stephan K. Galleitner
Mary O' Keeffe	Stephen Gilmer
Matt Hrushka	Steve Shipley
MIGHTY.CO	Susan Harman
Mother Sponge	tRavIs McCutcheon
Nate Spees	Victor Olade
Nicole L Morris	Wilson Galyean

CONTENTS

BRANDING IS FOR OLD-SCHOOL, MADISON AVENUE, CREATIVE-GURU, MARKETING GENIUSES

By Brant Cooper

Non-ROI-measurable marketing sucks.

Non-ROI-measureable marketing practices are a throwback to pre-Internet days, when advertising and branding were built upon a house of cards. Creative geniuses in their black turtlenecks mucking about in their black boxes creating "BRANDs" that turned commodities into classics, high school dropouts into gazillionaires, lemons into lemon meringue.

But they still exist. The House of Cards still exists. Why? Because sometimes it takes a long time to disrupt stuff. Piglets inside will do whatever they can to keep the house standing despite the foul stench of wolf-disruption breath. But the house of cards WILL fall, my friends, it will fall. When customer behavior is measured, advertising dollars WILL be spent on those practices that deliver return. Period.

Design geniuses already buy their faux eyeglasses online. And the marketers know it.

The traditional concept of branding is the last throwback.

"Where do you see yourself in five years?
What's your mission-vision-culture statement?
If you were an animal, what would you be?
If you were a dog, what breed would you be?
If you were an amplifier, how loud could you go?"

Pulse check: the World has Changed.

As Jeremiah argues, "your brand is your relationship with your audience." "Branding has always been about relationships," I hear you say. But we don't mean a customer's relationship with your brand. We mean the relationship IS your brand. Everything your business does AND doesn't do forms the relationship.

You used to broadcast your "relationship"; the engagement rules, the ethos, was communicated in one direction (message) and replied to asynchronously (buy/don't buy). As Patrick Vlaskovits might say, the medium was the message. The relationship was (perhaps subconsciously) heavily influenced if not determined by the medium (TV, radio, newspaper); the buying channel (high-end retailer, discount store, online, late night TV); and the volume (deafening, shouting, sotto voce, whisper).

This particular dynamic doesn't really exist anymore, other than perhaps with technology laggards.

Disruption strikes like a boa, but digestion takes a long time.

As if you couldn't guess where I'm going with this, the relationship between "brands" and customers has changed dramatically as the channel has changed from one-direction to multi-directional. It is both synchronous and asynchronous, it is both real-time and time-lagged, it is one-to-one, one-to-many, many-to-one, and many-to-many. You have to exist on multiple channels and prepare (if not invent) the next one. Your volume must match the ears of the market segment you seek.

Where's your creative genius to figure all that out?

Branding MUST be redefined to encompass the new reality. Brand loyalty is not simply based on logos, tag lines, and consistent messaging. Brandaneers will say "it never was," and then ask you what type of poisonous snake would you be in order to help you produce a color palette. It's always been about relationships, they'll say, as they bid to manage your social media stream and proceed to broadcast one-way "relationship" drivel.

"You will perceive us as such!"

Consumers are powerful and power-hungry. You will be crushed as quickly as you will be venerated. You'll reach the peak of the TechCrunch Bump, but just as quickly, the despair of the TechCrunch pit of "well that sucks, none of the those clicks were in our market segment."

So what is a "brand" exactly? And how are you going to evolve your thinking about the purposeful exercise of "branding"?

These are the questions that Jeremiah Gardner and I attempt to answer in *Entrepreneur's Guide to The Lean Brand*.

For startups, purposeful branding requires a deliberate effort to establish an ongoing relationship with customers based upon providing value. The brand must represent the achievable promise your business makes to its audience as delivered by your product or service, plus the shared aspiration you have with your customer to achieve change. In other words, your brand is a journey comprised of the utility of fulfilling a promise, plus the hope of achieving this emotional impact solving problems and fulfilling passions has on both you and your customer.

This is actually pretty heady stuff. And yes, if you're producing a "take-a-pill-and-be-wonderful" product, this isn't for you. But for those businesses built on or aspiring to create real value, you fit into this model, whether you're a startup, a small business, a life-style business, or a Fortune 1000 company.

Are you one of those?

And BTW, in this age of lean-everything, from diet meals to 'leaning-in' to introspection, a practice isn't lean because you say so. Nor is something "minimally-viable" because you say so. So no, you don't get value from throwing "lean" or "minimally-viable" in front of traditional practices.

Lean means eliminating waste. And just as with "lean startup," where you are attempting to eliminate the waste on building products no one wants, "lean branding" is about eliminating the waste of building a brand that no one wants a relationship with. In today's world, broadcasting the vision of your brand from the top of the mountain will be about as successful as the startup doing the same about its new killer iPhone app.

Whether incrementally improving an existing brand, re-branding your successful, long-standing enterprise, or building the next great startup, the winning relationship with your audience will come from a process of discovery. With this book, Jeremiah lays out a framework for you to study, practice and iterate on, and eventually make your own.

PART I:
THE SHIFT

CHAPTER 1

WHAT IS A BRAND?

SQUARE, BUMPY BOTTLES

Heineken is a well-known, global brand. When you think of Heineken as a brand, what do you think of? Global distribution, a distinctive logo, boring print ads, James Bond tie-ins, a green bottle, a customer base that supports a high-price point? That's how many branding experts would explain it.

There's another way to look at it, though.

Fifty years ago, Heineken made an interesting change to their bottles. They began putting their beer in square bottles with bumps on one side and dents on the other, almost like a Lego piece. They even brought in renowned Dutch architect N. John Habraken to design these bottles and called them the "Heineken WOBO" (World Bottle). Why a square, bumpy bottle? Was it better shelf appeal? Were the bottles more reflective of the "brand essence" of Heineken? Did Heineken commission a market research study that told them that younger people didn't like curvy bottles and preferred square instead? No. Heineken CEO, Freddy Heineken, on a recent visit to the Caribbean noticed two things about the poverty-stricken country he toured: the beaches were covered with discarded beer bottles and the people couldn't afford materials to build their homes. So he decided to manufacture beer bottles that could be turned into bricks.

The idea never caught on the way Heineken intended, and there are only a few existing buildings made of the bricks. But for a time, they made it easy for their customers to build whatever they wanted from their product and live inside. When customers fell out of love with the idea, the company moved on.

If this sounds like a great metaphor, that's because it is.

GETTING THE BRAND BACK TOGETHER

Let's start with a simple first step: defining terms. Any constructive discussion about brand development must begin with a clear definition of what a brand is. If you skip this step, you are more than likely to find yourself talking at cross-purposes, misinterpreting information, or arriving at faulty conclusions. Skipping definitions amounts to trying to recite the Gettysburg Address with a mouthful of peanut butter—although what you have to say may be powerful, no one is likely to understand it. Yet, a seemingly endless tide of definitions continue to be floated into the business lexicon attempting to define the term. None of these definitions are inherently wrong. None of them are inherently right, either. A small sampling of the many definitions for brand includes:

(in short form)

"A brand is a promise;"

"A brand is a trademark;"

"A brand is your positioning;"

"A brand is a gut feeling;"

"A brand is a brand name;"

"A brand is a perception;"

"A brand is your personality;"

"A brand is a set of expectations about you;"

"A brand is the essence of one's own unique story;"[1]

(in long form)

"A brand is what people say about you when you leave the room;"

"A brand is everything that the public thinks about you when they hear your name;"

"A brand is whatever your customers say it is;"[2]

"A brand is everything people see, hear, or feel about you;"

"A brand is a name, term, design, symbol, or any other feature that identifies one seller's good or service as distinct from those of other sellers;"[3]

"A brand is a singular idea or concept that you own inside the mind of a prospect;"[4]

"Brand is the image people have of your company or product;"[5]

"A brand is the intangible sum of a product's attributes: its name, packaging, and price, its history, its reputation, and the way it's advertised."[6]

For someone trying to grasp how to build a brand—much less understand what one is—that's a lot of peanut butter getting in the way.

To muddle understanding further, it seems we can't even agree on which part of speech a brand actually is. It is used as a **noun** when referring to surface artifacts (more on artifacts later) like a logo, a product, a visual identity system, or an advertising campaign. Brand is used as a **synonym** for "organization" when you hear people say things like, "The highest rated brand in safety," or headlines like, "Top-rated Brands in Cross-Channel Advertising Today!" If you replace the word *brand* with *company*, the meaning is unchanged. It's used as a **verb** when people say, "I need to brand," or "if we just brand ourselves," when talking about the need for, or work of brand development. The word brand is even used as a **possessive pronoun** (as in "our brand," "their brand," and "your brand") when comparing one organization against another.

With the rise in popularity for the term and the correlating clutter in our comprehension of what it means, it's no wonder our understanding of brand is, at best, murky. All of these misconceptions of what a brand is have diminished its potency and ability to create value in today's world—reducing it to a box on a business bingo buzzword sheet alongside the terms, "synergy," "core competency," and, "monetize."

Just take the recently leaked General Motors internal presentation as an example. In the midst of lawsuits, fines, government investigations and millions of recalls tied to faulty ignition switches connected to the deaths of at least 13 people, GM outlined, in an internal presentation, 69 words or phrases it felt should be avoided in any discussion of the (then potential) recalls. In the presentation, GM suggests alternatives like: instead of "bad," how about saying "below specification?" Don't say "defective," say "does not perform to design." Or instead of saying "safety" say, "has potential safety implications." To GM, this presentation was brand, and they are unfortunately not alone.[7]

Clever word play, spinning, distraction, an endorsement of minimum quality, million dollar ad campaigns, circumvention, and pricey deliverables have taken the place of the hard work of creating value with our brand development work.

WHAT A BRAND IS. HINT: IT'S A RELATIONSHIP

So, let's bring meaning back to the word brand and allow it to become powerful, potent, and value-creating once again.

A *brand* is a relationship between an organization and an audience.

A brand, by the very nature of how we interact with them, is a relationship. It may be a great relationship, or a terrible relationship, or a passionate relationship, or an indifferent relationship. But a brand is a relationship because it's how we, as humans, intuitively relate to products, organizations, and ideas.

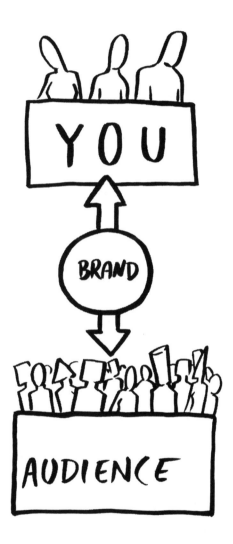

Relationships are the way we naturally engage with the world around us. We develop deep feelings, affections, biases, and associations with whom and what we choose to interact with and purchase on a daily basis. These feelings, affections, biases, and associations are best understood within the context of a relationship.

No matter what previous definition you tended to subscribe to, when we talk about a brand, what we're really getting at is relationship. Think about all of the various definitions listed above. A promise is part of a relationship, as is a name, perception, and personality. Relationship also accounts for what people say about you when you leave the room, as well as the intangible sum of a product's attributes. Expectations are part of a relationship as is everything people see, hear, or feel about you. The essence of a story is part of a relationship and relationship is definitely part of the image people have of you. All of these previous definitions boil down to one thing: relationship.

A brand exists *between* an organization and an audience because relationships are shared, not owned. All of the people, groups, and entities that form a relationship with you are part of your audience. Just like Heineken, you may have started your brand, but the rest of us have to live in it. All of your customers, employees, vendors, partners, sponsors, supporters, and competitors are part of an audience engaged in consigning meaning to your brand.

A brand only begins to have meaning with connection. That connection happens at the junction of who you (as the organization) are and who your audience (customers, employees, evangelists) aspires to be. Both the audience and the organization are simultaneously participating in a shared effort to attribute meaning to the relationship. To build value with your brand, you must see the relationship you form with your audience as the *synchronicity* between who you are and who your audience wants to become.

Thinking about brand as a relationship helps to clear up a lot of the murky water surrounding the term. We spend so much time interacting with brands on a regular basis it's no wonder we form relationships with them. We meet, we fall in love, and we settle down for life.

THE BRAND LANGUAGE ECOSYSTEM

Defining brand as a relationship organizes the language surrounding the term into a *brand language ecosystem*. When we use the word *branding*, for example, what we're really talking about is the work of relationship building. Or when we talk about *brand development*, we're really talking about the maturation of that relationship. Embracing brand as a relationship clarifies the meanings behind words that depend on its definition to begin with.

The Brand Language Ecosystem

> *Branding* is the aggregate effect of both the intentional and unintentional activities taken by the organization or the audience in establishing and maintaining their relationship.
>
> > *Intentional Branding* is the deliberate and conscious activities taken by an organization to project its value for the purpose of building the relationship with its audience.
> >
> > *Unintentional Branding* is the inadvertent influence on the relationship occurring regardless of intention as a result of action or lack of action.
>
> *Brand Development* is the maturation lifecycle of the relationship between an organization and its audience. There are three phases of development: brand-formation, brand-growth, and brand-management.
>
> > *Brand-formation* is the creation of the relationship in the early-stages of the brand's life.

Brand-growth is the scaling of the relationship post product-market-brand fit.

Brand-management is sustaining the already formed and scaled relationship over time.

A *Lean Brand* is a brand wherein an organization and audience have achieved a symbiotic relationship around common value without any extraneous activities.

When we use brand to mean a logo, visual identity system, product, or advertising campaign, we're only expressing a micro-meaning of a much bigger, deeper, and significant macro-meaning—the relationship. A logo, for example, becomes a shorthand expression of a relationship. A visual identity system becomes a tool for consistent transmission into a relationship. A product (or even a feature) becomes a direct expression of the relationship. And an advertising campaign becomes a temporary and targeted expression of a relationship, and so on.

The brand language ecosystem provides the foundation for how you begin to create value with your intentional branding efforts and gives potency, understanding, and meaning back to your conversations about brand once again.

CREATED, BUT NOT OWNED

Defining brand as a relationship helps you to understand brand outside of its many contextualized meanings. A relationship isn't a verb. We wouldn't say, for instance, "I need to relationship," or, "if we just relationship ourselves." Contextualizing relationship as a verb doesn't make any sense. Instead, you are able to use brand as a potent and much more meaningful noun.

A relationship is also inherently non-possessive. No one can own a relationship because it is inseparably defined between two parties (in this case, an audience and an organization). If you think about brand as a relationship, you can't talk about it being solely possessive. Instead, a brand is a shared entity with shared meaning. By definition, no one owns a brand.

The shared nature of a relationship also gives you a sense of bearing. No matter if you're an engineer, developer, right-minded, left-minded, creative, or scientific, everyone can relate to the concept of a relationship. This helps provide a common ground for understanding brand no matter what angle you might approach it from. We all have relationships. If you can relate brand back to the concept of your relationships, you'll be able to have a point of common contention to work from.

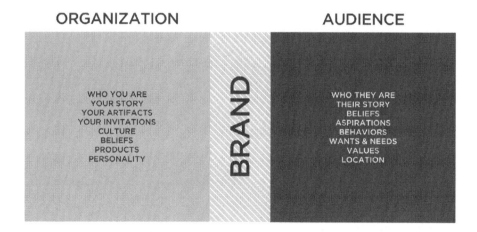

INCARNATIONAL, EVOLVING, EMOTIONAL

Defining brand as a relationship empowers you to understand the *incarnational* nature of a brand. Whereas brand lives both within the audience and within the organization, both parties are responsible for the ownership of the relationship. Brand, then, is present in every interaction between an audience and an organization as an omnipresent and ubiquitous expression of the deeper relationship.

It helps you to understand the *evolving* nature of a brand. Relationships are always in a state of constant definition and redefinition, transmission and reception. This is the human nature of business and the human nature of a brand.

It also allows you to understand the *emotional* nature of a brand. Relationships are with people; and people are sensitive, perceptive beings who develop deep feelings about who you are and why you matter.

RELATIONSHIP IS WHAT MATTERS

A brand isn't a logo any more than your friendships are phone numbers or street addresses.

It isn't a visual identity system, a product, advertising, a URL, and your brand isn't just what you say it is and isn't just what they say it is— it's both. Although these surface projections can signal people back to a broader capital "B" brand, they aren't a substitute for what a brand, in its most potent form, truly is—a relationship.

The importance we place on non-important things in brand development is astounding. All of the bells, whistles, glitz, glam, and cleverness are not the most important things. The most important thing is the real, living, breathing people you are forming a relationship with. When you understand brand as the relationship between you and your audience, you can stop placing so much importance on the things that don't matter, and start placing much more importance on the people who care about who you are and why you exist.

To bring authority and strength back to our understanding of what a brand is, we have to think about it as being synonymous with relationship.

Relationship is how we make sense of the world around us. Relationship is how we, as humans, relate to the products and companies from which we purchase on a daily basis.

Relationship is what matters.

THROWING DARTS

Over the course of this book, we'll explore a fresh approach to creating, understanding, and strengthening this relationship.

Much of this advice will run counter to the way you've been told brands are created. You will not find enthusiastic blanket endorsements of catchy tag lines, DIY identity guides, beautiful packaging, partnerships, clever positioning statements, Super Bowl ads, getting publicity, banner ads, following a hundred thousand people on Twitter, updated logos, street teams, celebrity endorsements, hiring Don Draper, or blogging until your fingers bleed.

After reading that list, you might wonder what's left. The answer is: everything.

Some of those things might work perfectly for you. The key, as you'll soon see, is to discover what your most enthusiastic audience is looking for, and testing every piece of your intentional branding effort at small scale to make sure you're right. If all you have is guesses, you're throwing darts, and you may not even have a dartboard yet.

Step one is developing a target and getting to know it. (And yes, this is still a dart metaphor.)

It doesn't take a genius to figure that out, no matter what you've been told.

CHAPTER 2

THE MYTH OF THE BRAND GENIUS

THE MYTH OF THE BRAND GENIUS

Most of us believe entrepreneurial visionaries are born, not made.

Our media portray business titans like Jeff Bezos, Richard Branson, Bill Gates, and Steve Jobs as heroes with X-ray vision who can look to the future, see clearly what will be, imagine a fully formed product or experience, and then simply make the vision real. Brant Cooper and Patrick Vlaskovits named this portrayal "The Myth of the Visionary."

In the Myth, the "Visionary" is a media-driven fallacy telling the story of the solo entrepreneur fighting his way through spasms of self-doubt, humiliation, genius, and torment at the hands of the ignorant hordes surrounding him. The Visionary (perhaps partnered with an eccentric) tinkers away in a garage until a Eureka! moment occurs and the world is changed forever, proving his vision from the onset.

There's a parallel myth to the Myth of the Visionary in brand development—*The Myth of the Brand Genius*. The "Genius" is the narrative of a creative recluse at the top of a Madison Avenue high-rise, who if given the right inspirational environment and paid the appropriate astronomical fee, will create a world-class brand over a long weekend.

The narrative creates a world in which a Genius' experience, knowledge, and brilliance are rewarded mightily with ensuing accolades from clients and peers alike.

The Genius promises to deliver a message that everyone loves, an identity that everyone relates to, and a strategy that can't be shaken. Then, it's just a matter of broadcasting those deliverables everywhere you can from Times Square to Tokyo.

Don Draper, the iconic lead character in AMC's *Mad Men*, captures the ethos of the Genius in one of his most memorable lines, "What you call love was invented by guys like me . . . to sell nylons. People tell you who they are, but we ignore it because we want them to be who we want them to be."[8]

The myth is so entrenched in our business culture, the popular publication *AdWeek* has an annual award they bestow to the "sharpest, brightest minds in marketing today," they call the "Brand Genius Awards."[9] Contrary to the romantic stereotype of the isolated Genius creating dazzling insights for the world to consume, the real world doesn't work that way.

Today, as much as traditional brand experts may flinch at the notion, the truly great brands are no longer being built on the 40th floor boardroom of an agency's "ivory tower." Nor do they come from in-house marketing departments pushing one-directional messages built entirely upon sales goals. Truly great organizations—with valuable relationships with their audiences—don't outsource their brand development and expect radiant results.

Instead, it's about converting your best thinking, astute ideas, and sharp hypotheses into facts rather than resting on a belief in someone else's "genius." To practice brand innovation, you must be open to the unknown, understand how to fail quickly, and value agile movement. Centralized Genius "command and control" simply doesn't work in an environment where innovation is the intention.

BRANDISM: THE GENIUS' BELIEF SYSTEM

Fueling the Myth of the Brand Genius is a set of underlying assumptions made about brand development across the board—from a first time entrepreneur's basement to the conference rooms of some of the world's leading agencies. Before we can address the root cause behind this "brandism," we need to dispel some of the misplaced and entrenched beliefs about brand development.

The Product Belief

The Belief: My product and my brand are one in the same. There is no distinction between the two. Good products create good brands. If I just work on creating the best product, I'll have the best brand.

The Truth: Products may have brands latent within them, but on their own, they aren't a brand. A product is an outcome of a much larger story. There's the team behind the product, the problem the product is trying to solve, the narrative of how the product came into existence. Not to mention the future customer support for the product, new features or accessories, and the trajectory of the company at large. There is so much more to a product than just the product itself.

You should be working to create an exceptional product. The product has to fulfill the promise that you are making to your customer to solve his or her pain. But stopping at the product alone truncates the story that is behind it. Stopping at product alone limits the potential relationship that an organization can have with an audience. It also limits the potential value that the product itself can have . . . but we'll get into that a bit later. Brand is everything else that goes into the product that isn't the product.

Products can be brands. Twinkies are a brand. The Whopper is a brand. But they also signal back to something bigger. Twinkies signal back to Hostess. The Whopper signals back to Burger King. Their value grows exponentially when connected to something larger than just the product itself.

The Rite of Passage Belief

The Belief: Brand development is for when my business "grows up." Right now, it doesn't matter. I'll deal with my brand when my startup grows up.

The Truth: Whether you know it or not, from the very beginning of your startup you are working with a brand. The minute you formed your business and started talking about what you wanted to accomplish, you created your brand. Every interaction you've had with either potential customers or paying customers has gone into shaping your brand. There is no rite of passage.

You may, in the future, have more resources (time, capital, knowledge) to put into developing your brand; but that doesn't mean that you have to wait. Waiting until you deem you're ready only complicates the problem rather than clarifying it. And worse, it can make things much more expensive down the line. Starting early and with intention can create value immediately that you can build on and grow from.

The Silo Belief

The Belief: Branding is just part of my advertising strategy and lives in my marketing silo or in the "customer relationships" block of my business model canvas. Branding is a marketing strategy, and my marketing team will take care of it.

The Truth: Your brand is everywhere. You may choose to file it under the large umbrella of "marketing," but the truth is it stretches far beyond the reach and scope of that umbrella.

Your sales team is articulating your brand. Your development team is creating products that can either build your brand or take away from it. Your C-level team is out proselytizing your brand. Your fundraising efforts are expressing your brand.

Brand is a part of every activity you are involved in as an organization and exists in every facet of your organization. It can't be quarantined off to the marketing silo and be expected to grow in value. Although there may be specific marketing campaigns that are geared around your brand's formation, growth, or management; your brand is much more than a marketing strategy. It's a way of life for your organization and a way of relating to your customers.

The Creativity Belief

The Belief: Creativity is the most important thing in developing my brand, and I'm just not that creative. I can't add any value to the brand development process; I'm the _____ [insert description] _____ (engineer, MBA, numbers guy, sales gal, intern).

The Truth: Creativity may be a part of brand development, but it isn't the gatekeeper to extraordinary brand development. No matter what you believe about your ability as a creative, you have a lot to offer to the brand development process. Your brand is about you. About your story and the unique attributes that make you who you are. No one else can tell that story but you.

You have to be willing to put in the time to articulate your story. All of the creative expressions of your brand start with an intimate knowledge about who you are, why you exist, and why you matter. Branding isn't a catchy slogan or a beautiful image, though everyone seems to think it is. The most creative and funny Superbowl spot ever isn't going to fix a second tier product or notoriously bad customer service. Even if you're the MBA, numbers guy or sales gal, you have a stake in your story.

The Control Belief

The Belief: I define my brand. My brand is what I say it is and will be received in the market as I envision it to be.

The Truth: As terrible as this sounds, your level of influence on how people receive you in the real world is, at best, 50%. Let that soak in for a second. Brand is the realm of relationship; and relationships are two-way streets. If you scream from the top of your lungs that you are the color red, but people see you as the color blue, you're probably some shade of purple and effectively blue.

Your brand is a shared experience between you and the people who chose to engage with you. You alone don't define your brand, but collectively (you + organization + team + audience) your brand becomes contextualized. You cannot divorce your brand from where it lives in the real world, and therefore, you don't have autonomy in what your brand stands for.

That's not to say you don't have influence. How you choose to express your story and how you choose to behave within this relationship has a significant influence on how you're perceived. But influence shouldn't be mistaken for control.

The Lottery Belief

The Belief: You have to win the branding lottery in order have an exceptional brand. Sometimes you're lucky; sometimes you're not. The chips will fall where they may.

The Truth: Brand development takes hard, intentional, and intelligent work. Even if there were a branding lottery, the cost of entry would be paid in blood, sweat, and tears. There is no such thing as pure luck when it comes to branding. Hindsight may create the illusion of luck for some of the organizations that have had success, but the truth behind that illusion is the amount of work that went into that success.

Successful brands are a mix of intention, iteration, time, and environment. No brand finds success overnight and no brand finds success without putting in the hard work it takes. Leaving your brand to simple chance is a sure way to lose a grip on the value you have to contribute in the world and whether your audience agrees with you or shares it with you.

The Emulation Belief

The Belief: My brand has to resemble my competition or the company I hope to become. If I want to be taken seriously, my brand should emulate those that came before me or those that are successful.

The Truth: No two brand-journeys are the same. They can't be. It's impossible. Simply emulating something else immediately violates the sanctity of your unique story. Void of your story, you certainly don't have a brand. One of every entrepreneur's greatest desires is to be taken seriously. Often that desire manifests itself in emulation. But copying others sells you short of creating your own value and your own place in the market.

Even worse, emulation is typically received with angst and mistrust. People feel the inauthenticity of an organization attempting to act like something that it isn't and will reject those things that are inauthentic to them.

Your brand is an expression of you. It's unique to who you are as an organization and the relationship that only you share with the marketplace. Chasing someone else's success can diminish what you could actually become.

The Design Belief

The Belief: My graphic designer or web designer will create my brand. After all, it does say "branding" on their website, or, I already have my brand . . . look at this awesome logo!

The Truth: Graphic designers, UX/UI designers, and web designers can be excellent at creating visual artifacts that point back to your brand . . . but they do not create brands. They simply reflect them. You should absolutely invest in great design when you're ready for that investment and you understand the value design will bring to your brand development, but chances are, you aren't ready for that yet.

The work designers do is only an expression of a much deeper story. Great designers understand this concept and can add immense value to your market proposition. Bad designers are simply misrepresenting what they are actually producing for you by calling their work "branding."

A brand is a multi-faceted relationship with your audience. Visual symbols are only a small fraction of what the totality of your brand actually is. A logo and letterhead do not a brand constitute.

THE INDUSTRIAL DINOSAUR

These Brand Genius beliefs produce run of the mill, generic, and ineffective brands. Even more, this type of thinking reduces the potential value your brand can create. As with all beliefs, they aren't imagined out of thin air. Instead, they are typically implanted in something much bigger and much more pervasive. To get at the root of the cause of this broken belief system, we have to trace it back to its roots—the industrial dinosaur.

The world today is defined more by Google than General Motors. We are in a period of human history characterized by a shift from an industrial mindset to a much more complex, connected, and social mindset. The exchange of information has become more valuable than the exchange of commoditized goods. Technology, information, and social connection have pushed us beyond our industrial limitations and introduced us to a new way of thought.

We are, undoubtedly, post-industrial.

Nilofer Merchant, author of *The New How* writes, "in the industrial age value was created through big institutions (i.e. IBM, General Motors, GE, etc.). They created products and services and dominated the business market. In the Social Age value is created though connected individuals. Passionate individuals are connecting around ideas which in turn are driving the creation of new businesses that are based on trust, authenticity and purpose."[10]

The differences are stark.

Industrialization centered around turning an extensive, complicated operation into a series of simple, repeatable, and automated steps. Big institutions had both the capital and manpower to turn the engines of the industrial machine. Through processes and consistency, they were able to dominate the creation of value through the mass production of goods.

The natural operational metaphor for industrialization is the factory. For a factory to work, it requires uniformity. Raw materials have to either already be uniform, or be quickly made uniform to simplify and accelerate tasks along the production line. Factories are based on maximum throughput (production), extreme uniformity, and streamlined processes.

The whole point of the factory was to create a product consistent in shape, size, composition, and aesthetic. Processed foods. Processing plants. Processing software. All are designed to take something imperfect and raw and turn it into something polished and uniform.

But things have changed. The world now centers around a revolutionary crowd dynamic. In our accelerated connectivity, individuals are instantaneously connected through millions of nodes throughout a vast network giving them the collective power to make decisions, attribute meaning, and determine value based on their connectivity. Through the organization of crowds, individual groups of people (not big institutions) are dominating the production of value throughout the world.

Manufacturing was at its simplest when you could have a Model T in any color as long as it was black. We've reached the polar opposite. The crowd dynamic has resulted in segments of customers being much smaller, requiring bespoke solutions. This is epitomized by digital fabrication where a custom product is only produced at the moment of demand. Whereas production and volume defined value in the Industrial Age, innovation and adaptability define value in the world today.

Sir Ken Robinson refers to this as "facing the revolution," where "new technologies are revolutionizing the nature of work everywhere. In the old industrial economies they are massively reducing the numbers of people in industries and professions that were once labor-intensive. New forms of work rely increasingly on high levels of specialist knowledge, and on creativity and innovation."[11]

There is no doubt this shift is real. The industrial mindset is a dinosaur.

THE OBSOLETE BRAND PROCESS

Which brings us to brand development. Brand development is almost exclusively thought about, taught, and practiced with an industrial mindset. To understand just how deep this connection is we have to go back to Promontory Summit, Utah.

In 1869 the Union Pacific Railroad and Central Pacific Railroad commemorated the United States' first transcontinental railway link at Promontory Summit by driving three final spikes into the ground (one gold, one silver, and one a mix of gold and silver). The "Wedding of the Rails," as it became known, marked the start of interstate trade.

Within a few short years, people's consumer choices were no longer constrained by the goods and products produced by their local economy. Instead, people were able to choose from a wider selection of goods from companies in a growing national economy. New products like canned food, the car, the electric iron, the vacuum cleaner, and the phonograph represented an extraordinary wave of life-changing innovation and choice for consumers.

As industrialization flourished, consumers were faced with growing choice. To cope, companies began using identifying marks (borrowing from cattle ranchers and both the Greek and Egyptian civilizations) on their products to indicate the source (or manufacturer) and to signal the quality of their products. As a result, the modern construct of branding, as a business activity, was born.

(Let this soak in for a minute—amidst the introduction of factories, assembly lines, and manufactured goods; our concept of what a brand is, how it functions, and most importantly, how we build them was formed.)

Promontory Summit was not only the "Wedding of the Rails" but also the "Birth of Branding" as we now understand it. It was natural for brand development to take the identity of the prevailing metaphor of the time— the factory.

In the metaphorical "brand factory," brand development was executed along a predefined set of principles, tools, and procedures used to produce a particular batch of deliverables that, in turn, were called a brand. Today, although we don't refer to it as a "brand factory," this predefined set of principles is better known as a "brand process."

Just like a factory, the brand process follows known cycles and step-by-step progressions based on a systematic series of actions. The outcome, in the brand process, assumes the equation will balance out to equal a brand. In shorthand, the process looks like this:

$$A + B + C = BRAND.$$

There are thousands of agencies with their brand processes mirroring this way of thinking. They may use differing language or seemingly proprietary ways of talking about the process, but at the core of almost every brand process, they are all the same. Even the concept of what a brand is gets boiled down to a set of deliverables: brand positioning, brand promise, mission statement, brand attributes, brand architecture, brand identity system, and so on.

If you've ever been through a process like this, you aren't alone. The linear process has trapped us in the factory mindset where we are blindly following best practices without firmly understanding the value being created. The brand process has reduced the powerful and unique relationship between an organization and its audience to a checklist:

Brand promise, check!

Mission statement, check!

Brand Values, check!

Logo, check!

Eventually . . .

Brand, check!

When you step back and see these processes for what they really are, you'll find the factory mindset hard at work in "brand equations" that look just like this:

[Brand Promise] + [Mission] + [Vision] + [Values] + [Positioning] +
[Attributes] + [Personality] + [Logo] + [Identity System] = BRAND.

This type of approach ignores how customers react to the brand. It does not differentiate between those who like it and those who love it. It does not involve appealing to a core audience, and acknowledging this brand may not be for everyone.

In the value-creation economy, brand development can't be about a process and can't rely on the factory—think of the twentieth century. As we witness every day, the result of these empty check boxes is carbon copy, manufactured, unimaginative, mass-produced, fabricated, and over-processed—frankly waste.

When it comes to brand-formation, too often we cling to the uncritical belief in a process. Too often the check box becomes more important than the real thing. Too often we think the process is actually what creates the brand. This type of thinking is obsolete.

THE MODERN LANDSCAPE

The end of the Industrial Age has shifted power to the consumer. The consumer now chooses the color, style, features, delivery time, and so on. Digital fabrication means the consumer is almost in complete control. While most products are not created this way, virtually all products have shifted toward that end point. It's the epitome of a lean approach: just in time, on demand manufacturing.

It makes sense, then, the relationships formed between an organization and an audience must also shift in this direction. It's a move away from the factory-mindset and toward a more fluid, agile, and adaptable mindset.

Great brands aren't strategically imagined ahead of time and can't be produced with factory precision. There are too many unknowns and too many ideas that have gone completely untested in the marketplace to contain your brand development within a process, especially in the startup phase of any business. Although no two brands are the same, all face the same challenge—deliver value or fail. Value is only discovered through experimentation, iteration, and innovation.

No matter what you've been told, what you've read, or what you've seen; there is no magic procedure, no silver-bullet, or thaumaturgic process that will produce your brand. Processes are great at producing manufactured, impersonal, and relatively predictive outcomes. But if you want to create real relationships with real value, you have to break from the manufactured, impersonal, and predictive outcomes.

To do so, we must make a shift.

THE SHIFT: LINEAR TO FLUID

The first shift is in moving our thinking from linear to fluid. A purely linear view of brand formation (A+B+C . . .) is less viable today more than ever in our past. Development based solely on selecting from existing processes and techniques is likely to be overwhelmed by changing forces in the marketplace, inside of your organization, or by forces unknown and unknowable to you at this point.

All brands, as relationships, are created by people and given meaning by people. As such, they need to be constantly re-created to survive. The ability to adapt and iterate is no longer a luxury, it is a necessity. Perhaps the most salient factor for the most successful brands of today will be their ability to innovate. Innovation can only happen with fluid modes of thought that allow you to draw from multiple places of learning to create depth, validity, and strength in the relationship you are building.

This is because there is no one way (or "right way" for that matter) of approaching your relationship with your audience in today's world.

Brand development is characterized by expansion and exploration in multiple directions. Rigidity is the enemy of great branding. Limiting your approach to your brand to a linear view eliminates the possibilities for exploration, growth, and discovery. The broader your thinking, the stronger your brand will be.

Steve Jobs, talking about Apple's brand-formation, said, "A lot of people in our industry haven't had very diverse experiences. So they don't have enough dots to connect, and they end up with very linear solutions without a broad perspective on the problem. The broader one's understanding of the human experience, the better outcome we will have."

Fluid thinking is much less constrictive. It weaves in and out of different thoughts and into unexplored spaces. As your brand develops, so do the needs of your thinking. Instead of adhering to a predetermined set of steps, fluid thinking allows you to jump from side to side, starting point to starting point, discovery to discovery throughout the development of your brand. Thinking in this way increases the possibilities for your brand to create value by allowing for exploration, discovery, and learning.

THE SHIFT: TACTICAL TO RELATIONAL

The second shift is in moving our approach from tactical to relational. In the conventional branding model, a brand is thought about as a one-way broadcast tool for organizations to tell customers about their offering. Branding, then, was primarily a tactical tool used to deploy information. Organizations manufactured information—logos, mission statements, color schemes, brand promises, campaigns, and so on—that broadcast their offering in a one-way conversation.

In tactical thinking, the four (or five, or seven . . .) "P's" (product, promotion, price, and placement) defined the information a brand pushed to its audience. But people can now compare features, prices, and promotions of dozens of similar products instantaneously and without much effort rather than rely on the organization to distribute the information they need. When consumers are empowered and able to speak up, it makes basing your branding around the tactical deployment of information irrelevant. Decisions about the four "P's" may still influence the way people perceive a brand, but they are no longer the most important decisions you have to make when it comes to your brand development. The more we try to play by the old handbook, the less and less effective it is.

Today, where information is relatively ubiquitous, people don't need an organization's help anymore to determine value. The tactical approach can no longer stand in an environment where customers' conversations, opinions, and reviews are instantly accessible. A company broadcasting its offering is no longer the only source of information for a consumer. The tables have turned.

That's why we need to shift our approach from tactical to relational. Branding is not about tactical genius. It's not about the clever thoughts of a few days' worth of thinking put through a "brand factory" assembly line. Today, branding is about discovering shared value in authentic, consistent, and intentional relationships with your audience. Branding success has been redefined as mutual prosperity, value, and respect—for shareholders, employees, customers, and communities. We must stop relying on deliverables to do the relationship building for us and embrace the pursuit of discovering shared value. Deliverables are about tactics; relationship is about value.

To make these shifts, we need new thinking, new language, and a new framework for approaching brand development. We need to learn how to test, measure, validate, grow, and create value with our brands in our new market reality. We need to bring entropy, energy, and life into the way we build relationships with people. In short, we need brand innovation.

That's why we say: **Brand, meet Lean.**

CHAPTER 3

BRAND, MEET LEAN

BRAND, MEET LEAN

The Lean Startup™ is a set of principles developed by Eric Ries and others, aimed at increasing the success of entrepreneurial endeavors by focusing on agility, validated learning, and iteration. The methodology centers around five core principles:

Entrepreneurs are everywhere—An entrepreneur is anyone creating new products or services in the face of extreme uncertainty and maximum risk.

Entrepreneurship is management—A startup is an institution, not just a product, so it requires management geared to its context.

Validated learning—Startups exist not to make stuff, make money, or serve customers. They exist so that people can learn how to build them into sustainable businesses.

Innovation accounting—Entrepreneurs need to focus on how to measure progress, how to set up milestones, and how to prioritize work.

Build-Measure-Learn—A feedback loop used to validate which business activities (including but not limited to product, distribution, delivery, marketing, and sales) in the marketplace are the right activities.

The Lean Startup methodology[12] has had an immense impact on the way entrepreneurs approach their startups. Most notably, Lean Startup has introduced language that restructures the way startups are taught, thought about, and approached. The significance of the language can't be overstated. It is the language that brings seasoned entrepreneurs together with first-time founders, giving legs to product innovations and creating value in the marketplace.

Although the concepts of Lean Startup aren't necessarily new, the way they are being applied has opened new territory in innovation and product development. Lean Startup borrows from lean manufacturing, as represented by the Toyota Production System.[13] Simply put, lean manufacturing is about optimizing efficiency in all value-added (providing value to customers) activities and eliminating all non–value added (not providing value to customers) activities.

Let's be clear: Lean does not mean small, cheap, limited, or sparse. Instead, it focuses on the streamlined creation of value for both the final user of a product and the internal customers who link activities throughout the product's development and delivery.

For all of the incredible conversations and real impact the lean methodology has created around product innovation, **the role that brand plays** has been glaringly missing.

BRAND VS. PRODUCT, PRODUCT VS. BRAND

Product is only part of any true market proposition. Customers rarely know, much less care about, the development process you went through to create your product. Yes, we need to create great products that solve real problems. Yes, these products should be validated in the actual marketplace. And yes, we need better product experiences.

Yet it is impossible for a customer to have a product experience without having interacted with brand. The product, as the tip of the spear, is often the first interaction with brand. To neglect intentional branding is to walk away from the opportunity to capture value from all customer interactions that aren't your product. As a result, you are leaving on the table the opportunity to define the shared aspiration that is necessary for high growth.

If you strip down your product to only the problem it solves, what do you have left? Where can people connect? How do people become passionate about you? This is a question too few founders have asked themselves.

Products evolve, teams transition, and markets shift, however, what's at the foundation of any organization's success is the relationship they can (and should) have with their audience. This is brand. Without value-creating brand, there is no relationship.

The good news is your brand already exists. Whereas business development is heavy lifting and technology development is splitting atoms; brand is good news. Like any relationship, it's a breath of life. Sure, brand needs to educate, engage, and delight your audience; but unlike civil engineering, the roads between people are already there, hidden under the lightest layer of dust, waiting to be connected. But if you can't articulate what value you offer that no one else can, you don't have a grasp on what your brand is and the potential it has to offer.

The first challenge, then, is to recognize that your brand development isn't controlled or dictated by a Brand Genius or some silver-bullet process. This means you are no longer buying into any of the misplaced brand beliefs fostered by the "brand factory" process outlined in Chapter 2.

The second, and more daunting, challenge is to retake control of your brand and become intentional about its development, growth, and sustainability. To retake control, you must work to co-evolve the development of

both product and brand in connection with one another in an effort to
discover the value-creation potential your business has.

Enter the Lean Brand Framework.

By mapping Lean Startup principles to brand development, we can create a new framework for building sustainable, validated, and passionate
relationships with our customers based on shared value. The Lean Brand
framework places a new paradigm of brand development in the hands of
startups and organizations that are ready to experiment, validate their
hypotheses, and build long-term relationships with their customers.

LEAN STARTUP + LEAN BRAND: A SUCCESS STORY

An Interview with Joel Gascoigne (Cofounder and CEO)

Buffer is an app that allows you to create and share your social media content across platforms on your own schedule. You can click the Buffer button on any website, and your content will be scheduled for an ideal time on Twitter, Facebook, and other social sites. Buffer is a shining example of a real Lean Startup success—going from MVP (minimum viable product) to 1.5 million users and $3.6 million in revenue in three short years. (To read more about Buffer's journey, I highly recommend the blog series called "Building Buffer.") Joel Gascoigne, founder and CEO of Buffer, shares the Buffer story and his thoughts about applying lean methodologies to brand development.

TLB: Tell me the Buffer story. Where did the idea come from?

I started Buffer from the UK. I spent a year and a half on a previous startup called OnePage before I began working on Buffer. In both cases, with OnePage and Buffer, it was a personal need/personal pain point I was solving.

TLB: How did what you learned from OnePage carry over into your approach to Buffer?

The big mistake I made with OnePage was to assume that meant it was just going to work. I didn't validate to find out if other people also had that pain point and whether it was a big enough pain point to build a business on. So I spent a year and a half on OnePage, and ultimately it wasn't too successful, but that's where I learned a lot of lessons that carried forward.

Then, with Buffer, I decided I needed to approach it in a much more lean way. One of my biggest goals was just to be able to get to a point where I could work full time on my own startup, on my own project, and that was the goal I approached Buffer with.

TLB: Tell me more about how you used "lean" to build your audience with Buffer.

With Buffer, I ran two different MVP landing-page tests with no product. The first one was just a two-page website. A landing page and then you would click "Sign up," and it would take you to a page that said, "We're not quite ready yet, but give us your email, and I'd love to let you know when we are ready to launch." That was great because the first page made it look like the product actually existed. So, I got a lot of validation because the only way to get to that page was to actually click "Sign up." After the first test, I had a lot of conversations with people via e-mail, then a couple of Skype calls, and I did quite a bit of relationship building there.

The second test was whether or not people would actually pay. So I reworked the website's flow to be: landing page to "Pricing and Plans" button and then to an actual pricing page with three plans—free, $5/month, and $20/month. People would then have to pick one of those plans to end up on the page that said, "We're not quite ready yet." We had lots of conversations resulting from that test as well. I collected 120 emails in those seven weeks, and on the first day of launch about 50 people signed up. These are not huge numbers, but it was kind of working.

TLB: So you ran a smoke test to gauge whether people would be intrigued and even hopeful before you built out the first version of the product?

Yeah. I mean, nothing can be completely validated, but that helped a lot and made a big difference to have people say, "If this existed, I would use it; if this existed, I would pay you for this." Then I went ahead and built the first minimum version of the product.

Three days in, the first person started paying for Buffer. That was just a huge moment. It was only $5, but it was just huge, a big moment. That payment and the next few payments, I was jumping around the room. This was completely different from making money any other way.

TLB: Absolutely. How did those first 120 emails you collected and your first paying early adopters lay a foundation for your brand development?

Those initial relationships actually set the tone for a key part of the Buffer brand formation, because the way I approached those first few conversations was based on wanting to get as much information as possible from the conversations in order to validate whether people would want to use the product and whether it would be successful.

With that in mind, I approached them very, very personally. People got a very personal email in their inboxes from my email address, and I tried to share insights into the development process and how it was going, building out the product. Once we launched and people started signing up for the paid version of Buffer, we continued that very personal communication style.

I think we found right away that people really loved that. Of course, it has to be genuine if you want to take that approach, and it was. That was what we really tried to aim for. So with the first handful of paying customers, as soon as they started paying for Buffer, I was really intrigued, and I wanted to learn who these people were and what was the key value they were finding in Buffer and why they wanted to pay. I would always just click through to their Twitter or their email address and click through to their website just to see what each person was all about.

There was one guy who was a photographer. I clicked through, and he had a website for his photography with some amazing photos. I remember I ended up on a really awesome photo, I think it was some kind of landscape or sunset. I just casually mentioned that photo in the email I sent him and said, "Welcome to the paid plan. I saw your photography, and I really loved this photo."

I think people really picked up on that genuine interest, and it became very compelling. That is something that has become a key part of our brand as we've grown.

TLB: How has that impacted the way you've approached building your audience now?

Now we're at 1.2 million users and $3.9 million annual revenue with about 17,000 paying customers. We've been lucky in a lot of ways and we've figured out a lot of things along the way. It feels like we are at a good point right now and growing fast.

We have some pretty ambitious goals we set for ourselves in terms of how great of service we want to provide. Right now about 80% of emails we receive get a response in one hour and 95% get a response within 6 hours. We are pushing to improve on that and eventually our highest goal is to do 95% within one hour.

That's been a key part for us and it has helped us, we get so much feedback, and people really love that. If you search Twitter at any point for Buffer, generally you will find people that are really happy with the service and raving about it. I think that helps our brand overall.

So we've tried to reinforce that relationship by doing things like including at the bottom of every email we send, "PS You Can Reply to This Email," because a lot of times people have a "No Reply" email and we don't do that with any of our emails. You can reply with anything about Buffer or if you just want to say "hello" and we'll reply back very quickly. Sometimes we have people that reply back and just wanted to test to see if they actually are going to get a response from a human.

TLB: In your opinion, what makes lean so important for brand development?

One way that I think about brand is you can be known for a few different things and I think great brands, eventually are known for many different things. For us customer service is one we have always worked on really hard. The other one has always been creating great content because we just did that from early stage. (My co-founder) Leo's key role for the first year was that he wrote a lot of great articles and we got very well known for that. That is the way we've ended up building an audience. Our brand has emerged as a result of the efforts we put into building our audience in a sustainable, lean way.

FOCUSING ON WHAT MATTERS

First, the Lean Brand Framework gives you a way to distill your brand down to its most important elements. It eliminates the unnecessary waste found in conventional branding processes and allows you to minimize the amount of time and resources needed to succeed in the marketplace. Speed, agility, and adaptability are key to building a successful brand today.

The opportunity cost of focusing on the wrong things in branding is high. When you focus on the low value tasks, you are not focusing on the tasks that will eventually and directly create value for your customer.

At an early stage of development, you shouldn't be concerned with all of the clever ways you want to project your brand to the world. Rather, you should focus on how your customers react to your intentional branding and how your customers relate to you. Facilitating, measuring, and understanding these reactions are the basis for discovering and creating value with your brand development.

GET OUTSIDE YOUR BUILDING

Second, it forces you to get outside of your building (or garage, co-working space, or 35th floor high-rise). Planning, strategy, devising, outlining, meeting, scheming, and calculating made up the majority of your activities in the old model. But these activities keep you trapped inside of your building, and worse, take you away from physical proximity to the people that matter the most—your audience.

The Lean Brand Framework takes you outside of your building and puts you where your relationship will develop the most—in front of your customer. In today's rapidly changing marketplace, organizations that get in front of their customers and learn to listen have a significant advantage over their competitors.

YOUR FOUNDATION FOR GROWTH

Third, it gives you a strong foundation for growth. As everything you do within the framework has to be measurable, you will understand quickly what works and what falls flat. This gives you a powerful engine for validated growth. The framework is designed to help you focus on your strongest emotional-value offering first. You can expand your story, artifacts, and invitation once you've validated the value you are creating for your existing audience and convert it to provide a strong, sustainable brand platform serving as a foundation to invest in new offerings.

Growth in this way allows you to become adaptable to the needs of your customers over time. The framework gives you space to diagnose and repair parts of your brand development that aren't working and accelerate parts that are working. Adaptability provides a more accurate and direct validation of how your brand resonates with your audience.

Not only does the Framework provide a foundation for your growth, it can make the work you're already doing as a startup much more valuable. In any lean endeavor, the aim is to discover the value you're creating. Brand will fundamentally be a part of this discovery. If you're already using lean methodologies in your product development, Lean Brand techniques can only enhance and bolster the value you will eventually create.

Before you begin your Lean Brand work, there are two important distinctions to understand—*value ecosystems* and the *innovation spectrum.*

VALUE ECOSYSTEMS: EVERYTHING IS INTERCONNECTED

Everything in an organization is interconnected. You can't go about the business of developing a brand without taking into account the product, the customers, the distribution channels, the business model, the production cycle, and so on. The inverse is true as well: You can't go about the business of building great products, business models, production cycles, and so on without taking into account your brand development.

Everything is interconnected.

Do you remember playing Jenga or pick-up sticks as a kid? Pulling one stick out of the pile might unsettle all the others. In the same way, there are three interconnected and vital parts working together to establish a value-creating organization—*product, culture,* and *brand.*

One part can't be removed without disturbing the whole and undermining the capacity and strength of an organization's value-creation potential. Which means an organization must live within a *value ecosystem* wherein products, culture, and brand work in concert to deliver value to its audience. Keeping the entire ecosystem healthy isn't child's play, it's a fragile game of company survival—hyper-focusing on or ignoring any element affects everything.

In nature, the ant colony demonstrates the interconnectedness of value ecosystems. Is it the worker ant (product) going out to gather food and ward off enemies who is most important? If everyone in the hill were a worker ant, how successful would the colony be? Is it the nurse ant that tends to the eggs (culture) who is most important? How many generations of future ants would exist without food and protection from competition, let alone more eggs to tend, if every ant was a nurse ant? Is it the winged Queen, laying eggs and starting colonies (brand) who is the most important element of an ant ecosystem? Surely the ability to start colonies is the most important element of ant success! But how does the old saying go? "Too many cooks spoil the broth." Of course, it's not the worker, egg-tender, or Queen who is most important—it's all three that gives the colony the ability to survive, grow, and thrive.

All the resources, abilities, and relationships interconnect to determine an organization's value-creation potential. Products create functional-value. Branding creates emotional-value. And culture creates the impetus for both product and brand. All three are fundamentally and inextricably interconnected to one another. In turn, an organization's business model must also accommodate and recognize the interconnectedness of these resources, abilities, and relationships throughout this ecosystem.

Any reduction or neglect of any of the elements of the ecosystem affects the whole. Growth in all three areas is needed for the ecosystem as a whole to progress and evolve or all the others are held back as one unit and the whole suffers. Moving forward as a value ecosystem is a gunny-sack race, not a baton race, and not a solo marathon or sprint.

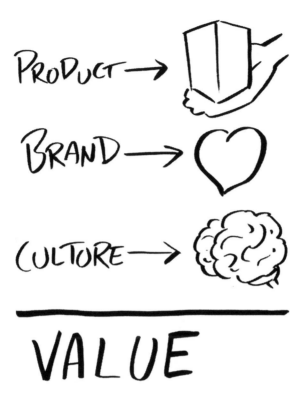

In terms of business models (or books, articles, opinions, methodologies, and the like), the purpose of focusing in on one aspect—product, culture, or brand—is to understand the role each plays in the whole. In other words, successful organizations do not rely on value to the customer being delivered only via one aspect, but rather all three are integrally involved.

Once you zoom in to understand how one element creates value, you must zoom back out to understand how it impacts the other elements. No one aspect alone creates the totality of value for the organization.

When it comes to brand, we zoom in for the purpose of understanding the unique value that the relationship between the organization and the audience brings the audience.

Brand is *always* in service to the ambitions of the overall business. Brand isn't the end point and isn't a synonym used to refer to the overall organization. A brand doesn't exist independently from the overall business.

The iconic Kodak brand achieved branding "nirvana" in their cultural ownership of the phrase, "Kodak Moment." Yet, the failure to evolve their products with emerging digital technology ultimately lead to Kodak's well documented fall from grace. Pan American Airlines owned an iconic brand known for the possibilities and escapism of jet travel. Yet, Pan Am's failure to evolve its product offering, specifically their reduced flight routes and services, forced the company into bankruptcy. You can make the argument that both Kodak and Pan Am still exist as cultural placeholders, but you can't go as far as to argue that they still create value.

No matter how clever and powerful a brand is, it can't sustain long-term value on its own independent from the ambitions of the overall business. Brand is *always* in service to the entire business, not just itself. (We wouldn't say customer service is the business, nor would we say the distribution network is the business, though those could be its shadow force.[14]) In the same way, the brand *isn't* the business; it's a part of it.

The same goes with products. Products that solve problems are great, but not accounting for the emotional impact—without corresponding aspiration—the product will die on the shelf. Yes, Apple Macintosh products were more elegant, stable, and user-friendly in the 1990s than PCs, but product superiority didn't win because end user satisfaction didn't factor into the purchasing decision. What mattered to IT Managers, whose jobs were on the line, was increased organizational productivity vs. the cost of the equipment.

The same is true of culture. Culture is the way an organization relates to itself. How employees talk to one another. How they collaborate. What they value as a group. How they get things done. From the brand perspective, it's the relationship employees—from the CEO to the delivery truck driver—form with the organization.

Culture creates value for an organization's audience because it is the impetus for both product and brand value. The purpose of culture isn't in increasing productivity, making your employees happier, becoming the envy of your competitors, or possessing the ability to attract top-tier talent alone. All of these outcomes are great, but are proxy measurements of a much bigger end result—delivering value to your audience. Passionate employees will more than likely create passionate customers. If the culture is laggard, or there's lots of infighting, or if the "value aspiration" of the sales team isn't aligned with the service team, it will adversely impact the value delivered to the audience. On the other hand, if the culture is strong, the value delivery (and creation potential for both product and brand) to the audience is strong.

Take Zappos for example. Their product allows you to safely buy shoes that you like and that fit online. Their brand delivers happiness via amazing customer service, randomly upgrading shipping, and their personal care of each customer. Their culture is the impetus for both. People love working at Zappos because they empower their employees to use their imagination to make customers happy, use "cultural assessments" rather than performance evaluations, and a laundry list of other reasons. Product, brand, and culture are all interconnected in the way that Zappos delivers value to their customer.

There's one more dimension that is core to all three—product, brand, and culture—which we will discuss at length in Chapter 5. That core dimension is simply what Simon Sinek calls the 'WHY.'[15]

Why do you, as an organization, exist? Why did the founders come together to create this entity? No great company was founded on the basis of desiring wealth. They are founded on the desire, need, passion to make a dent in the world. Why did you form your entity? For what purpose in the world does the entity exist? Why should employees come on board (*culture*)? What problem do you promise to solve (*product*)? What aspirational impact will that have on your customer (*brand*)?

Brand agencies and geniuses would like to believe brand is the end point just as much as engineers and product managers would like to believe product is the end point. Both are wrong. Customers don't experience an organization in disjointed brand, product, or culture silos. Instead, they experience the value an organization offers through the aggregate of everything the organization does to deliver that value.

Everything is interconnected.

THE INNOVATION SPECTRUM: SUSTAINING VS. DISRUPTIVE

Drawing on patterns of innovation in a variety of industries, Harvard Business School Professor Clayton Christensen introduced the concepts of sustaining and disruptive technology. In *The Lean Entrepreneur,* Cooper describes *sustaining innovation* and *disruptive innovation* as end points on a spectrum—the *Innovation Spectrum.*

A disruptive innovation is an innovation that helps create a new market, eventually disrupting an existing market. In disruptive innovations, both the market and the value that is being created are unknown. Ford's Model T was a disruptive innovation because the mass-produced automobile changed the transportation market. The automobile, by itself, was not.

A sustaining innovation doesn't create new markets, but rather evolves existing ones with better value, allowing the organizations within to compete against each other's incremental improvements. In sustaining innovations, the increased value that is being created might be known or unknown but the market is well understood. Samsung's Galaxy S5, which directly claims significantly better battery life over the iPhone 5, is a sustaining innovation.

SUSTAINING   DISRUPTIVE

BRAND DEVELOPMENT LEADS THE WAY	PRODUCT LEADS THE WAY
PROBLEM WELL UNDERSTOOD	PROBLEM NOT WELL UNDERSTOOD
EXISTING MARKET	UNKNOWN / NEW MARKET
INNOVATION IMPROVES DIFFERENTIATION	INNOVATION IS DRAMATIC
INCREMENTAL CHANGE	RADICAL CHANGE

Generally, large, successful businesses occupy the sustaining end of the spectrum; university programs, large company labs, and R&D centers occupy the disruptive end. Startups tend toward the more disruptive side, but fill the entire spectrum. To succeed, an organization *must* move toward the sustaining end. The sustaining side represents where the big market is.

As a general rule of thumb it's helpful to understand this distinction: sustaining innovation comes from listening to the needs of customers in the existing market and creating products that satisfy their predicted, felt, or projected needs for the future. Disruptive innovation creates new markets separate of the mainstream—markets that are unknowable at the time of the product's conception and are initially too small to 'be interesting' to large established firms.

The Innovation Spectrum provides an important foundation for innovation of any kind, including intentional brand-formation. The amount of intentional branding outside of the product increases as you move from right to left. If you tend toward the disruptive side, the initial brand-formation evolves primarily from the product itself. Other elements are less important: Facebook's lack of a real logo, a company name like Google, no tech support, and so on. On the other hand, if you tend to the sustaining side, you have to be able to position yourself within an existing market—what differentiates you—via something beyond simply the product's features and benefits.

The reasoning behind this distinction comes back to viewing your value offering through the lens of your audience. Truly disruptive products inherently have a disruptive story, and therefore can pursue disruptive relationships. The more disruptive you are, the more the initial relationship between the organization and their audience is realized within the product and through the insights, people, and drive behind creating the product.

Although Xerox has since expanded into workflow software, document management, scanners, and information technology outsourcing, the market that the Xerox 914 (their first photocopier) created clearly defined the relationship they built with their audience. Even today people still say, "Can you make a Xerox of that," when referring to a photocopy.

On the other hand, the more sustaining you are, the more the relationship with your audience will define your intentional branding efforts. If you build a business around a commodity, say cereal or eyeglasses or a "me too" product, then non-product brand-formation becomes your differentiation.

Sustaining innovations are joining the noise of a well-established industry or category. Customers have already formed relationships and expectations about that category. That's where the differentiation from category competitors is the foundation of your brand-formation. Your audience's willingness to receive you is dependent on the relationship.

From the outset of your venture, it's tough to know exactly where you fall on the spectrum. In truth, your initial guess will be your best gut feeling as to where you land between the sustaining and disruptive sides of the spectrum. If your entire startup is a department your biggest competitors don't even have, you probably tend toward the disruptive side. If you're creating a new market, you probably tend toward the disruptive side. If your innovation is dramatically different than anything that currently exists in the market, you probably tend toward the disruptive side.

On the other hand, if you find yourself identifying your product with "me too" language (We're fast-er! We're cheap-er! We're sleek-er! We're new-er! We have great customer service! We are more interested in design! We are more personal! Our product looks a little different than our competitors!), you probably tend toward the sustaining side.

No matter which side of the spectrum you may fall, or how strong your value ecosystem is; it's important not to confuse what makes a brand successful in the short term with what makes it successful in the long term. In the short term, a brand needs either a disruptive product or differentiated relationship to survive. It needs to be early in a new category or highly differentiated in an existing category. But in the long term, as the disruption moves quickly toward the sustaining side, product differentiation becomes more difficult to discern. What's left is the difference between your brand and the brand of your competitors.

These two distinctions—the value ecosystem and the innovation spectrum—are vital to the way you approach your Lean Brand work. Throughout the rest of this book, we will reference these two ideas continuously in the principles, concepts, and work within the Lean Brand framework.

Ready to get to work?

CHAPTER 4

THE LEAN BRAND FRAMEWORK

THE LEAN BRAND FRAMEWORK

The Lean Brand framework is designed to work in parallel with the Lean Startup methodology. It is intentionally optimized to get the most out of the activities you are already doing and employing while building through lean techniques. On its own, the Lean Brand framework is a tool for brand innovation. Together, the Lean Startup and the Lean Brand provide a dynamic platform for value creation, business model discovery, and the development of an exceptional, sustainable business.

With each phase of work inside the framework, your brand will become more realized and add to the overall value potential of your organization. In between these phases are large **gaps** posing challenges for a startup to overcome. For your brand development efforts to create value, you must cross the gaps to "**get to the other side.**"

To help illustrate these gaps more clearly, meet Pixelriffic.co—a hypothetical startup founded by co-founders Ben and Brooke with big dreams of changing graphic design software. They've built a cloud-based design software that allows people to create designs for Web or print including blog graphics, presentations, Twitter covers, flyers, posters, and invitations. Throughout this chapter, we'll follow Pixelriffic through their

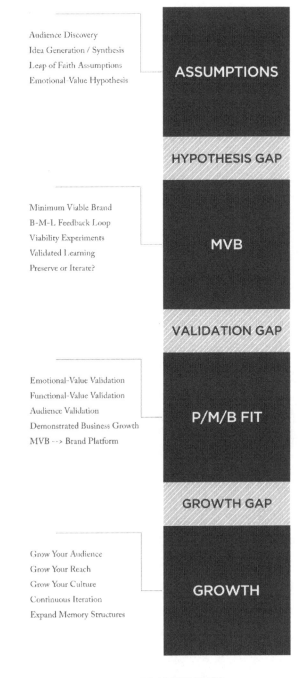

Audience Discovery
Idea Generation / Synthesis
Leap of Faith Assumptions
Emotional-Value Hypothesis

ASSUMPTIONS

HYPOTHESIS GAP

Minimum Viable Brand
B-M-L Feedback Loop
Viability Experiments
Validated Learning
Preserve or Iterate?

MVB

VALIDATION GAP

Emotional-Value Validation
Functional-Value Validation
Audience Validation
Demonstrated Business Growth
MVB --> Brand Platform

P/M/B FIT

GROWTH GAP

Grow Your Audience
Grow Your Reach
Grow Your Culture
Continuous Iteration
Expand Memory Structures

GROWTH

THE LEAN BRAND FRAMEWORK

hypothetical Lean Brand journey to see how the framework would apply in a "live" setting.

GAP 1: THE HYPOTHESIS GAP

The first gap is the *hypothesis gap*. Every company begins with a set of assumptions formed prior to ever writing a single line of code or of a business plan. These assumptions create the fundamental beliefs a startup will begin to experiment with and learn from. The knowledge gleaned forms the basis of future growth. In the context of a brand, this is no different. Brand development begins with assumptions about who you are, why you will matter, what people desire, like, think, believe, want, and ultimately will become passionate about.

To cross the hypothesis gap, you must frame your ideas, guesses, and hunches as a set of assumptions and evaluate those assumptions to form an emotional-value hypothesis you can then test. You will know you've crossed the hypothesis gap when you're able to first test your ideas with an initial audience to generate feedback. Assumptions should be based on well-formed ideas, developed from industry knowledge, expertise, and instinct. You can split this into two parts—*idea generation* and *idea synthesis.*

Idea generation is about a no-holds barred approach to generating a quantity of ideas. For assumptions to provide actionable places to start, they must conceptually explore the opportunities present. During idea generation, a startup may use different levels of ideation such as Design Thinking™, structured exercises, observation sessions, or mind mapping to evaluate and compose its initial assumptions.

You can use a simple set of "quick fire" questions to spur your idea generation:

1) *What business are we in / want to be in?*
2) *Why do we think it matters? Why do we think people will care?*
3) *Who do we think will be most passionate about our story?*

Once you've generated as many ideas as you can, you will move on to idea synthesis. Idea synthesis is the comparison of these ideas against one another to form a set of assumptions. You'll want to compare and contrast your ideas against one another to determine which are the most integral and which aren't. After sorting through your ideas to arrive at a set of assumptions, a startup has to decide which assumptions to test. The ideal is to test the most critical assumption first. The most critical assumption is that assumption that is the least known (there are no analogs in the market, for instance) and if not true, obviates the need to further test the idea. In other words, is a deal-killer. In *The Lean Startup*, Eric Ries refers to these assumptions *leap of faith assumptions*.

There are two essential assumptions every startup has to make: the *value hypothesis* and the *growth hypothesis*. As Ries put it, "these give rise to tuning variables that control a startup's engine of growth. Each iteration of a startup is an attempt to rev this engine to see if it will turn. Once it is running, the process repeats, shifting into higher and higher gears."

EMOTIONAL-VALUE HYPOTHESIS

To form a Lean Brand, your value hypothesis must expand to include your leap of faith assumption about the emotional-value you will create. This assumption forms the premise of your emotional-value hypothesis from which you will explore and learn.

We will talk more extensively about the difference between emotional-value and functional-value in Chapter 8, but for now, it's useful to understand their implications on your hypothesis. The *functional-value hypothesis* describes the value created in solving a problem for your customers. The *emotional-value hypothesis* describes the value created in the relationship your customers will form with you (for example, helping your customers reach their aspirations, customers becoming passionate about you, and the impact solving the problem has on the customers' lives.).

Functional-Value hypothesis + Emotional-Value hypothesis = True-value hypothesis.

You may choose to treat these as independent from one another or you may choose to integrate them into one. What you intend to build and the audience you intend to develop will drive how you treat your value hypothesis. Much of this decision will be based on your best thinking about where on the innovation spectrum you fall. Remember, if you tend toward the sustaining side, your intentional branding efforts must work to differentiate you in a known market; whereas if you tend toward the disruptive side, your intentional branding efforts must follow the product's lead.

For example, if you intend to offer a physical product on the sustaining side, it makes the most sense to integrate them as one. A sustaining physical product directly engages the customer using the product in a known market. Packaging, placement, physical look and feel, and product color are all part of the product experience and the brand experience. A startup would struggle to test their physical product with the value hypotheses independent from one another.

On the other hand, if your product is purely digital and tending toward the disruptive side, it may make more sense to test the emotional-value hypothesis independent from the functional-value hypothesis. Although overlap always exists between the two, the functionality of the product and the branding elements may need independent measurements to be accurate and generate learnings from which to build.

No matter how you decide to test, a startup has to measure progress against a high bar: *validated* evidence a sustainable business can be built from its product and brand. You can only assess this standard if you have made clear, tangible hypotheses ahead of time. In the absence of putting a stake in the ground, product and brand development decisions are far more difficult, time-consuming, and less accurate.

It's best to actually write your hypothesis down so you can refer to it and iterate on it later down the development line. You can use a structure like this:

We believe [this set of people] will [care / be passionate about us] for / because [this reason].

Over at Pixelriffic, Ben and Brooke have generated a ton of ideas using some design thinking techniques. Their initial ideas revolved around a discussion about how design is becoming more and more important today. They believe everyone wants the designs on their blogs, posters, or websites to look professional; but that most people don't have the skill or the money to use the expensive, complicated software that professional designers use. These are all great functional-value assumptions—if they are able to build an easier, cheaper way for people to create professional looking designs, their product will fill a functional need for an audience. But these are not emotional-value assumptions. To begin to understand why people would become passionate about Pixelriffic, Ben and Brooke had to go deeper.

What emotional impact does making design simpler and cheaper for the average person have? What world view does only Pixelriffic offer to an audience that no one else can? Where will people "light up" when they learn about their startup? They distilled their ideas about these types of questions down to one critical assumption—that their fight to make design simple, accessible, and cost-effective meant a world where every idea can be beautifully presented and where people will feel more connected to an artistic part of themselves. If this assumption doesn't connect with their audience, then there is no need for them to continue down the path of development.

Their hypothesis came out like this:

We believe people who value great design will be passionate about Pixelriffic because making design easy and accessible gives our audience the ability to connect with their artistic side and turn their ideas into beautiful designs.

Not only does this hypothesis get beyond the functionality of Pixelriffic, but it gets to the heart of what makes them unique: they can help people connect with their aspiration to be artistic and turn their ideas into reality. If people connect with them here, they have a good shot of building a strong relationship with a core audience. If they don't, then they need to go back to the drawing board to reshape their next hypothesis.

Assumptions are springboards for exploration and experimentation. They are the starting points for you to begin testing in the marketplace. To test the value you will actually create in the market, you must work to develop the best value hypothesis you possibly can. The quality of your hypothesis will determine the potential learning you can glean from testing.

GAP 2: THE VALIDATION GAP

The next gap is the *validation gap*. To eliminate waste in the discovery of value, a startup has to resist the temptation to simply start building final versions of its branding elements based on its assumptions. Instead, you must move from your emotional-value hypothesis into a phase of learning and validation to discover what works and what doesn't. To cross the validation gap, you must empirically prove the value your intentional brand development efforts are creating through *validated learning*. To do so, you must experiment.

In the Lean Brand framework, experimentation is facilitated through an iterative *Build-Measure-Learn feedback loop* testing a *Minimum Viable Brand (MVB)*. If an element in your MVB works, keep it and prepare it for scale. If it falls flat, iterate and test again. Crossing the validation gap is demonstrated by business growth and the formation of a passionate group of customers. The MVB is the vehicle to cross the validation gap, and you want to build on the elements that work and iterate on those that don't until you find *Product-Market-Brand fit*.

MINIMUM VIABLE BRAND (MVB)

A *Minimum Viable Brand (MVB)* gives a starting point for your intentional brand development by distilling your brand down to the most critical elements—*story*, *artifact*, and *invitation*. You will work to develop your first iteration of your brand by articulating your story, creating your first artifact, and learning how to invite people to join you with your first invitation. With time, there are likely other pieces that may surround these elements, but from the start, these three elements are the crux of what really matters to your customers.

As you begin to build your first MVB, keep in mind that each of the components are meant to be prompts to inspire the development of the overall relationship. They are not meant to be checkboxes requiring completion, but instead a diving-in point to begin building from (to that end, in we've put together a tool to help you in your MVB work called the *Minimum Viable Brand Canvas*. We'll explain more on how to use the canvas in Chapter 12). Part of the uniqueness of an MVB is that it concentrates your brand offering down to the essential parts needed to enable a full turn of the Build-Measure-Learn loop with a minimum amount of effort and the least amount of development time. Although an MVB is agile, to successfully start testing you have to find both the *minimum* and *viable* expressions of each of these components to get through a full Build-Measure-Learn loop as quickly as possible.

Don't over-invest too early or you run the risk of creating a lot of waste without understanding what resonates. In the same token, don't under-invest in the development of your MVB or you may not get the level of feedback you need to generate data to get to validated learning. Every startup has to find the balance between these two terms within the context of what they are creating, who they are creating it for, and where they intend to test.

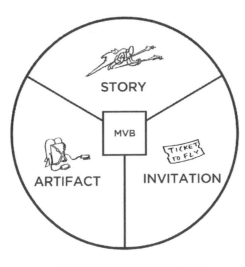

MINIMUM VIABLE BRAND

Let's talk about the components of an MVB in a bit more detail:

Story

Story is the scaffolding for your relationship with your audience. You want people to hear your story and be compelled to become part of it, have a deep emotional connection to it, and share it as if it were their own. The story gives voice to who you are as founders, who you are as a startup, why that matters, and what kind of organization you want to build. You need to know your story intimately, believe it yourself, and be able to communicate it concisely and compellingly in order to build an audience. In Chapter 5, we'll explore the power of stories and dig into how to build an authentic story.

Artifact

Artifacts are expressions of your story. Whether it's a pink mustache on the front grill of a car (Lyft) or a set of golden arches outside of your building (McDonald's), the goal is to find artifacts that project your story and engage people in a memorable way. They can be either temporary (an experience or event) or permanent (the Google campus or the tattoo of your startup's motto on your arm). Artifacts should reflect your relationship with your audience, collectively project your story, and build a strong memory structure for your customers. In Chapter 6, we'll talk about developing artifacts that create engagement and interaction in detail.

Invitation

Invitations are the mechanisms to ask people to join you on a journey toward shared value. Invitations are much more than simple marketing messages. The context, medium, content, and structure of how you invite someone to join are all important. The right invitation can be the difference between achieving satisfaction and passion from your audience. In Chapter 7, we'll look at how to form compelling invitations and how to evolve them throughout the growth of your relationship.

Measuring Impact

Although deceptively simple, creating an MVB requires extra work. You must be able to measure its impact. For example, it is insufficient to build an MVB that is evaluated solely based on your team's internal preferences about design, look and feel, or other subjective-based judgments. You also need to get it in front of potential customers to gauge their reactions. Testing requires you to get outside of your building and either validate or invalidate your assumptions in a "live" setting. This enables you to close the divide between your assumptions and reality.

Any brand development work that is based solely on the subjective opinions of a marketing agency, a group of executives, or a few team members is insufficient. The relationship people form with your startup has to come at least horseshoe close to the reality they are going to experience. Otherwise, you can end up souring relationships with both early adopters and future customers, which will stunt your potential growth (or worse). This is why using successive MVBs to validate the relationship you are forming with your audience is crucial to your brand-formation.

Crossing the validation gap is about experimentation and validated learning. You shouldn't be worrying about your first hundreds and thousands of customers or statistical significance. You want to validate the relationship you are building with a core, passionate audience first. Every activity you choose in regard to your brand should be intensely focused around learning as much as you possibly can, as fast as you can possibly learn it. Unlike conventional branding, where you start with heavy "market research," creating robust deliverables, putting together sweeping "brand strategies," and trying to appeal to the masses; planning works in reverse order in a Lean Brand:

1) What do you need to learn?

2) How will you measure to know if you are gaining validated learning?

3) What do you need to build to run an experiment and get a measurement?

Use your Minimum Viable Brand as your experimentation vehicle. In retrospect, you will more than likely (and should) be embarrassed by your first MVB. Don't get stuck on the details. Keeping this in mind can relieve you from feeling like you need to have a finished, neat, and polished branding effort. Instead of focusing on polish, your efforts should focus on helping your customers believe that you comprehend who they are and care about their relationship with you.

With an MVB, you're creating the groundwork for the relationship you hope to develop with your audience and providing your customers with an initial interaction point. Through experimentation, your MVB will eventually become the strategic foundation of your brand.

Let's check back in with our co-founders at Pixelriffic. Working from their value hypothesis (and after reading Chapters 5, 6 & 7), Ben and Brooke have worked to develop their first MVB. Their story's genesis comes from their shared belief, as designers, that there is value for their audience to get in touch with an artistic part of themselves. They hope to help people achieve this aspiration by enabling them to turn their ideas into beautiful designs in a simple, accessible way. They've found that they're fighting for people who, just like them, believe that great design doesn't need to be complicated or expensive.

They've chosen their first artifact to test: a simple landing page that tells their story with the colors, typography, and shapes they decided on. They've included an invitation for people to join them by asking them to download the "Pixelriffic Manifesto" (a poster they designed using Pixelriffic that says, "I, _____, will turn my ideas into reality through design. I will trust my instincts, let curiosity guide me, and let my designs tell my story"). In fact, their first experiment will more than likely be to track how many people download their poster, print it out, fill in their name, and take a photo of it to share on Facebook.

Ben and Brooke have put their MVB together in a simple, agile way to allow them to start testing with their audience. They're ready to launch their first experiment.

BUILD-MEASURE-LEARN FEEDBACK LOOP

At the core of a startup's experimentation is the Lean Startup's *Build-Measure-Learn feedback loop*. Although the loop was initially introduced as a tool for product innovation, it is an incredible tool for brand innovation as well. In the Build-Measure-Learn loop, the point is to generate validated learning wherein an organization is able to learn in the marketplace in order to base decisions, actions, and accountability around the knowledge learned.

As customers interact with your MVB, they will generate both qualitative feedback (for example, where they connect and where they don't) and quantitative feedback (for example, how many people participated or how many people shared your content). Both are important to uncovering insights throughout your brand development. For the feedback to be beneficial, it is important—no matter if you have an established relationship or are developing a new one—to think of your organization as a learning organization first. That means the primary function of your team is to learn from your interactions with customers rather than building polished versions of your branding elements.

The mechanics of the loop are straightforward. The first action is to enter the build stage as quickly as possible with an MVB to test. The second action is to measure the relational traction your Minimum Viable Brand creates through viability experimentation and metrics to track the impact of your effort. The final action in the loop is to learn from the data generated and validate or invalidate the emotional-value hypothesis along with the pieces of your brand that are working and iterate the pieces that aren't.

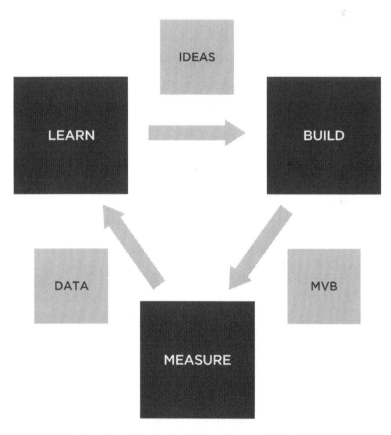

BUILD-MEASURE-LEARN FEEDBACK LOOP

Every iteration on your MVB merits another round of audience feed-back. As you experiment and move your MVB through successive Build-Measure-Learn loops, you'll need to adapt based on what you're learning in your testing, all in an effort to discover and validate the value you will create for a specific market.

If you are building the wrong thing, optimizing the artifacts of the brand will not yield significant results. Just like if you're building the wrong thing, optimizing your channels or your message won't yield significant results. Instead, once you can validate the relationship you are building, then optimization will yield growth results.

In Chapter 8 and Chapter 9, we will dive into the emotional-value metrics of interaction, engagement, and participation to understand how to measure within the Build-Measure-Learn feedback loop. The Build-Measure-Learn feedback loop is designed to help you generate learning and facilitate your journey toward discovering Product-Market-Brand fit with an audience.

PRODUCT-MARKET-BRAND FIT

At its simplest, product-market fit refers to being in a strong market with a product that can satisfy the functional-value needs of that market. But simply satisfying the needs of a market doesn't go far enough. To build a sustainable business, a startup must also find fit in how its branding is creating emotional-value. This is called *Product-Market-Brand fit* (PMBF). In The Lean Brand framework, you must expand your thinking about product-market fit to include the emotional-value you're creating through the relationships people are forming with you.

Finding fit with a market with both your product and brand is fundamental for a startup in order to achieve growth. At its core, product-market-brand fit is about finding synthesis between who you are, what need your product is promising to address, and how your customers emotionally relate to you (in other words, how your brand fits).

Ideally, finding Product-Market-Brand fit will be a unified effort wherein validation can be demonstrated in relative succession or in junction to one another. But this may not always be the case. Products are short-term value creation whereas brand is long-term value creation. Clarity around your brand and how it relates to your overall value creation is also critical to creating accelerated upward trajectory for a growing startup.

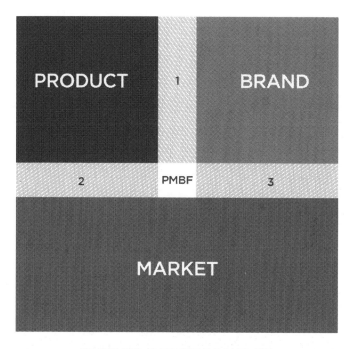

PRODUCT-MARKET-BRAND FIT
1—*Product-brand fit* means you are the right people to build this product.
2—*Product-market fit* means your product fulfills
the functional-value needs of a market.
3—*Brand-market fit* means being in a strong market with a relationship
that can inspire passion around its emotional-value offering.
Center—*PMBF* (Product-Market-Brand fit) means not only do
you know how the product fits within a certain market, but
you also know how the brand fits with that market.

It's important to continue operating in an integrated mindset. Don't give in to the temptation to separate the brand from the product or the product from the brand. Instead, the closer you can keep them together, the more synchronized they will be, and the more overall value they'll create. The farther apart they are, the less synchronized they will be, and the less overall value they'll create. The best strategy is to find synchronization between product, market, and brand prior to growth.

Remember Pixelriffic's first experiment (the "Pixelriffic Manifesto)? Ben and Brooke learned a lot from that experiment. They found that daily bloggers really connected with their story and loved the ability that Pixelriffic gave them to create great designs both quickly and affordably. To their surprise, professional designers didn't seem to connect with them (which was a valuable discovery because they didn't have to waste their time trying to compete with the likes of Adobe, Apple, and Microsoft). They have made their first discovery on their way to finding Product-Market-Brand fit.

We will talk more extensively about PMBF in Chapter 11, but product-market-brand fit is a benchmark in your business development marked by real, measurable growth. Finding Product-Market-Brand fit is always demonstrated by positive improvements in an organization's core metrics and signifies the start of your growth phase.

GAP 3: THE GROWTH GAP

The final gap is the *growth gap*. This phase of work in the Lean Brand framework is transitioning from experimenting with successive turns through the Build-Measure-Learn feedback loop with an MVB to forming a *validated brand platform* from which to scale. A brand platform, in a Lean Brand, is built from the validated learnings you've gained in your MVB.

To transition, you must move from your emotional-value hypothesis to your *growth hypothesis*. A growth hypothesis has to test how to create external demand to grow the depth and scope of relationships with your audience without adversely affecting existing value.

Once you know the value you are creating through your story, artifact, and invitation elements, these pieces form the understructure from which you can grow your audience, grow your reach, and grow your culture. We will talk at length about forming your growth hypothesis and brand-growth in Chapter 10. Your growth is generated around your best thinking about how you can scale your intentional branding efforts to attract, engage, and form relationships with new customers.

After continuous experiments, learnings, and iterations on both their MVP (minimum viable product) and their MVB, Pixelriffic was growing to the point that they hired their first 10 employees and moved into a bigger building. What they discovered through their experiments with both their product and their brand has led to measurable positive growth. That positive business growth, over time, signaled they had found product-market-brand fit with their first passionate group of customers—food bloggers.

Through their Lean Brand work, they knew how they created value for their audience, which was demonstrated by the continuous and growing passion they received from the food blogging community. They have successfully built their brand platform. Now they need to start figuring out how to grow. Do they push into new markets (like the craft beer industry or the Reddit crowd)? Do they change their business model to create premium and freemium users? How should they grow? These questions tell Ben and Brooke that they're ready to move on to their growth hypothesis. Although they've found initial success, the road to accomplishing their big dreams is still evolving. They must learn to expand their team, expand their reach, and expand their culture in order to build the business they envisioned from the beginning.

FRAMEWORK VS. PROCESS

Before you dive too much deeper, it's important to be clear about what is meant by the word *framework*. A framework is a loose and flexible structure that leaves room for other practices, ideas, and tools. The Lean Brand framework is intended to serve as a support or guide for the development of your brand, which expands and grows as you expand and grow.

Unlike a process, nothing is untouchable or "checked off" in the development flow. Everything is a hypothesis until verified in the marketplace.

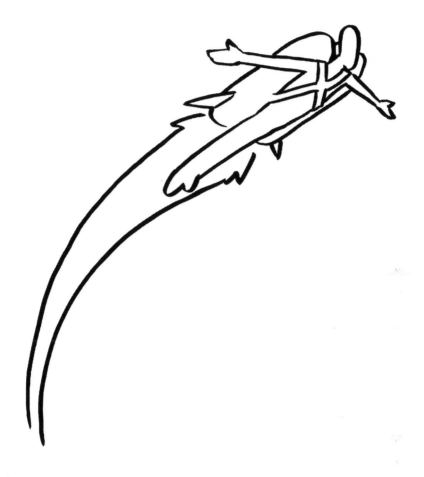

This means all of the activities in your brand-formation are hypothesis-driven. Working within a framework is much more compelling than a linear process when it comes to brand innovation, because if what you're doing isn't working, you can't declare yourself as having crossed the finish line.

You can think of the framework as a "sandbox" to play in. It will guide what to look for and where to focus while being flexible enough to adapt to changing conditions, new discoveries, and breakthrough insights. Your research, hypotheses, and experiments throughout your brand development will flow from the sandbox, determining what you will measure and what types of validation you will look for.

Remember, a process excels at manufacturing uniform, impersonal, and predictive outcomes. Flexibility, agility, and validated learning are vitally important within the Lean Brand framework. In fact, this is the basic principle of the framework: not having to reinvent the wheel every time you face an iteration or growth cycle.

In the short term, the Lean Brand framework gives you a way to start right now. In practice, it forms the foundation for your brand's formation while the components of the framework form the foundation for iteration. The Lean Brand framework does away with foreboding, low value added tasks (for example, the creation of generic surface assets like mission statements, brand promises, and color schemes) in order to fully focus on the value-creating development tasks of your brand as it relates to your customers.

In the long term, the framework ensures the durability of what you build. It helps identify what information is needed to sustain an effective brand and provides insight into how to iterate and grow as needs change and your business grows.

Anything that does not directly create value or intentionally build the relationship you have with your customers is wasteful. The goal is to eliminate waste in the discovery, creation, and delivery of value.

Throughout the rest of the book, we will explore the Lean Brand framework in depth. In **Part II: Build**, we show you how to create value with the different elements of your Minimum Viable Brand: story, artifact, and invitation. In **Part III: Measure**, we will talk about emotional-value at length including the discovery of your value stream, establishing relational metrics, and provide ideas for brand-centric viability experiments for you to run. In **Part IV: Continuous Iteration**, we will talk about growth, show you how to apply Lean Brand principles to existing brands in the enterprise, and present the Lean Brand Stack with specific tools for your intentional brand development.

For your efforts to succeed in service to building the business you envision, or to help your existing brand to thrive, you must be willing to experiment and fail in search of the right relationships with the right audience.

Now that we've covered the basics, let's dive in.

STORY

ARTIFACT

TICKET TO FLY

INVITATION

PART II
BUILD:
MINIMUM
VIABLE BRAND

CHAPTER 5

STORY

THE FOURTH EARL OF SANDWICH

British aristocrat and statesman John Montagu loved playing cards. He spent most of his free time around the card table attempting to best his opponents with his skill. As the story goes, late one November night in 1762, the Earl was hours into a marathon poker game and couldn't be bothered to leave the table for dinner. He asked a nearby servant to bring him a piece of meat and two slices of toast. To leave one hand free for his cards, he placed the meat between the two slices of toast and, as John Montagu was the fourth Earl of Sandwich, what we know now as the "sandwich" was born. He may not have been the first to eat meat between two slices of bread, but nonetheless, we still borrow his name every time we order a sandwich.

Beyond being fodder for your next trivia night, the origin story of the sandwich gives us insight into why storytelling is so important. If you had simply been told the sandwich was created by John Montagu in 1762, you'd probably never remember the information. Yet when the information is placed within a story, your chances of forgetting the origin of the next sandwich you eat are pretty slim.

Stories are powerful.

Academy Award winning novelist and screenplay writer Larry McMurty once reflected, "If, for example, you dare to interrupt a five-year-old's

thirty-ninth viewing of 'The Lion King' in order to find out a basket-
ball score, they will, once they regain control of the remote, immediately
rewind the film to the point of interruption, so as not to miss the smallest
element of the story. Watching the avidity with which the very young
absorb stories . . . leaves one no grounds for pessimism about the survival
of narrative itself. The human appetite for it is too strong."

Story is the first piece of your Minimum Viable Brand. It is the backbone
of any relationship because it has the ability to engage, delight, and relate to
an audience in a way that nothing else really can. Stories are enduring links
to our shared cultural traditions, knowledge, myths, and symbols. They
have been carved, scored, scratched, painted, scribbled, printed, burned and
inked onto wood, bamboo, ivory, bones, pottery, clay tablets, stone, skins,
bark, paper, silk, canvas, textiles, film, and electronic hard drives all in an
attempt to connect us to something much larger than ourselves.

ONCE UPON A TIME

Aspiration is our strongest driver of behavior. It is the drive to fulfill our
dreams and to live a deeper life. We all have aspirations. Some aspire to
greatness, or aspire to beauty, or aspire to do good. Aspiration invites passion. By engaging a person's aspiration with your story, you invite others
to be passionate about you. Nike engages our aspiration to be a better athlete, and athletes are passionate about wearing Nike products. Patagonia
engages our aspiration for adventure, and adventurous people are passionate about Patagonia.

If people are simply satisfied with you, you'll struggle to grow. To get
to passion, you must tell a story that resonates emotionally to engage your
audience's aspirations.

Think about your Netflix queue. You probably have a long list of movies
and shows you want to see, and for most of us, near the bottom are some

highly praised foreign films, documentaries, and maybe a few National Geographic shows. You never get to them, because you keep putting *House of Cards* and *Archer* at the top of your list. When people set out to create other products, they often want to create something that looks like and sounds like everything else. But that's a good way to end up down at the bottom of the queue and not get watched. You want to be urgent. You want to be the thing people hear about and think, "I will get this one *next*." To generate the level of emotional connection you need to become "next" in your audience's proverbial Netflix queue, you must embrace telling your story.

Jonathan Gottschall, author of *The Storytelling Animal* writes, "Humans simply aren't moved to action by 'data dumps,' dense PowerPoint slides, or spreadsheets packed with figures. People are moved by emotion. The best way to emotionally connect other people to our agenda begins with 'Once upon a time . . .'"[16]

Let's talk about *your* "once upon a time."

WHAT'S YOUR STORY? (YOUR "ONCE UPON A TIME")

What's the first thing you do when you meet someone new? You ask them to tell you their story. You ask them where they're from and what they do. You ask them about their family and their friends. You ask them what makes them laugh and what their aspirations are. When people first meet one another, they naturally ask each other to share a piece of who they are in an attempt to find the initial sparks of common ground from which they can relate to one another. There is nothing more human than sharing a story with another human being.

The same is true for brand development—great branding starts with your story.

But what is "your story?" Is it you as a founder? You as a startup? You as a collective of employees and your office bulldog? Just as Shrek, the iconic character voiced by Mike Myers said, "Ogres are like onions. Onions have layers. Ogres have layers. We both have layers." Startups are like Ogres (and onions) too. All startups have layers that work together to form a compelling story for your audience.

These layers provide the basis for defining who you are as a founder, who you are collectively as a startup, why that matters, and what kind of organization you're working to build. Although there are probably hundreds of layers that go into a story, there are two pieces that are vital to your Lean Brand work—the *founder story* and the *startup story*. As you begin to define the different layers of your story, keep in mind that they must work together in unison in order to tell a unified narrative for people to connect to.

THE FOUNDER STORY

Behind Google was Sergey and Larry, behind Intel was Gordon and Robert, behind Virgin was Branson. Behind every startup, there is a *founder story*. The founder layer is the genesis from which your startup will grow. Founder stories are not personal brands. In fact, personal branding is a myth unto itself.

The point in your founder story isn't to create an alter-ego called your "personal brand" that presents a super-human, polished, and robotic version of the real you. The point is to be authentic in telling the audience what purpose drives you, and intentional about how that story is communicated.

Ask yourself, Why are you here? What got you here? Why you are the one to do what you're doing? Do you want to change the world? Do you want to make your former classmates jealous? Do you want to meet Elon Musk? What makes you get up in the morning? What change do you want to see in the world? Probability suggests you will find yourself somewhere between making a decent living and Tom Hanks in Castaway. Are you okay with that? If you can't answer these questions, your customers are certainly not going to do it for you.

You have a story to tell, and it deserves to be told well.

Although your founder story includes your passion, it isn't solely what you're passionate about. Whoever said, "do what you love and the money will follow," missed the mark. If you don't fill a customer's need or solve an urgent problem from the start, you've already lost, no matter how passionate you may be. Passion alone won't ensure your success because passion without a profitable and sustainable market is a dead end. You may be passionate about 13th century feather pens, but if no one is interested in buying those pens, you're sunk from the beginning.

That's why the best stories start with you as a customer with a need, not you as someone who's hoping to profit from filling that need. It's not enough to simply say, "I always wanted to run a bagel shop," or, "Since I was young, I've been passionate about starting my own tech company." These types of stories fail to connect to anyone.

Instead, ask yourself what you're committed to. What point of view are you committed to? What change in the world are you committed to? What problems are you committed to solving? Commitment means effort, and effort is what leads to success.

Your founder story is your electrical current. It's the fuel to keep driving you onward. When what you are deeply committed to, what only you can bring to the world, and what turns the economic wheels of your organization forward come together, your work, life, and impact begin to move toward greatness.

THE STARTUP STORY

Every organization focused on growth eventually evolves beyond its founders. Although Elon Musk's story as a founder is rooted in SpaceX as a company, SpaceX has a story all its own. As customers begin forming a relationship with the startup itself, your story must evolve into a collective *startup story*. Naturally, events will build, milestones will pass, and your startup will take on a life of its own.

Is your startup story a tale of David vs. Goliath? Or is it an idealistic narrative of a better future? Is it about adventure on the high seas of technology or an aspirational drama reaching for greener pastures? The secret to forming passionate relationships with your audience starts with one thing and one thing alone. It's not positioning. It's not the right mix of spellbinding words. It's not your logo, your brand "essence," your placement ads, your vision statement, or a proprietary agency process.

It starts with your **aspirations** as a startup.

It starts with your ability to be clear about what you aspire to change, solve, or do and why that impacts your audience. Your startup story isn't about the simple who, what, when, or where; but about why your organization exists and what you aspire to become. Chronology matters much less than telling a story that follows an interesting arc. Your founders, employees, stakeholders, and those invested in the success of your organization must understand the startup's unique and authentic story; and learn to tell it well. Sit back and analyze. Take out a pen if you need to. What detail will you lead with? What should you emphasize? What will you leave out? What does that leave you with? Why?

Great companies don't settle. They fulfill their aspirations from a deep understanding of who they are, not from positioning, products, placement, or price. It's this aspiration that will have people lining up around the corner to join you, and it's this aspiration that has to be captured

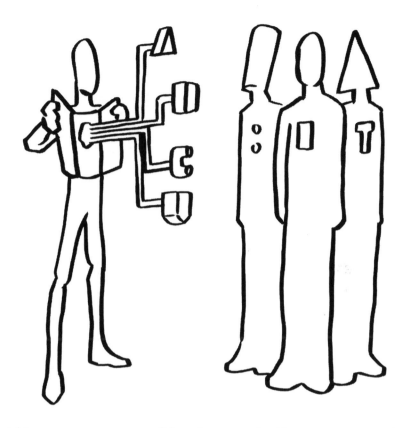

within your startup story. More importantly, if your customers don't understand your aspiration, they have no reason to ever care about what you do or how it might benefit them. They have no reason to connect with you. The relationships people form with organizations don't solely come from a great product or having great customer service. Instead, relationships come from inviting them to something much bigger.

Your startup story, and your customer's ability to see themselves in it, is the reason people will become passionate about you. Absent a compelling connection to your audience, your startup will quickly become white noise, drowned in branding jargon, and deemed irrelevant by your customers. Not only do customers care about the company's story, but they care deeply about how they fit into the story.

TOMS Shoes got its start with founder Blake Mycoskie telling the story of one-to-one philanthropy and invited people to give back with every purchase they made. That evolved into the story of TOMS as a company and gave people a clear way to see themselves in it.

GoPro started when founder Nicholas Woodman went on a surfing trip and couldn't find a high quality yet inexpensive way to film his experiences. As they grew, GoPro found success by enhancing the emerging action sports industry and helping the average person become the leading character in their own videos.

Charity:Water started when founder Scott Harrison, while volunteering in the developing world, realized that all their efforts with education, medicine, and safety weren't going to get anywhere without clean water. As the organization grew, Scott's story evolved into a story of about clean drinking water and offered people a chance to donate their birthday to help people suffering from a lack of clean water. To this day, you can still donate your birthday to the cause of clean drinking water.

Just like TOMS, GoPro, and Charity:Water; knowing your story, being confident in it, and providing room for people to see themselves as a part of it are crucial to your brand-formation. Sharing the struggles, wins, challenges, ups, downs, rights, lefts, bumps, bruises, and victories is more important now than it ever was before. People want to know who they're supporting and why they should care.

Tell people the truth and allow them to see your organization's aspirations.

The point in telling your startup story is not to present your audience with a polished and exaggerated version of who you are. Stories don't magically turn crappy products into good products, just like great direct response marketing or advertising or PR don't turn crappy products into great products. Instead, you must both make great products *and* learn to tell your story in a compelling way.

Don't treat your story as marketing glitter to sprinkle on top of your product. Your story is a powerful tool for connection with your audience. Leave the aggrandizement, exaggeration, and gibberish alone. Your startup story will create value when you're able to communicate your aspirations in an authentic, real, and relatable way. That's where people connect. That's where people engage.

No matter your endeavor, you should always think of yourself as an instrument for storytelling. Every organization, big or small, has a story to tell. And that story is unique to you and has the potential to allow you to engage with your audience in a very human way because it's rooted in the reality of how people really think and really act.

As Jim Signorelli, author of *Storybranding*, writes, "Stories don't create our beliefs. Rather, their themes are like magnets that find and attach themselves to beliefs that already exist. Additionally, the best stories amplify the importance of existing beliefs by charging them with emotion. Telling someone that war sucks conveys the information. Showing someone how war destroys the hopes and dreams of innocent people conveys the same information with power."[17]

Both your founder story and your startup story are driving forces behind your MVB. They are the foundations upon which both your artifacts and your invitations are built. To build successfully, you must take ownership of communicating who you are in a compelling and real way to bring people to the core of who you are.

To do so effectively, you must free your story from the confines of a static vision statement; you must break out of the *feature bubble* to get to the *WHY*; and you must establish a *rally point* for your customers to begin to see how they fit.

VISION STATEMENTS ARE OVERRATED

It's likely at some point in the life-cycle of your startup a potential investor or partner will ask you about your company's vision statement (or brand promise, or mission statement). Despite the fact many business management experts and branding experts alike argue a vision statement is the cornerstone of your brand strategy, **vision statements are overrated.** Too many founders spend way too much time and create way too much waste attempting to write a splendid and altruistic vision statement that, in truth, never creates any real value in the market.

In reality most startups will not be able to fulfill their vision statement no matter how well written it is. Market conditions, mergers, acquisitions, growth rates, trends, production issues, and so on have direct implications on your ability to actually deliver on your vision statement. For a startup, where high-risk and high-uncertainty abound, building your story from a vision statement is like planning a wedding without ever going on a first date. If you lead with a grandiose vision you can't deliver on, you've tainted the relationship from the beginning.

Most vision statements are full of bland truisms and blasé business jargon making them anything but informational, powerful, or inspirational. People aren't inspired when they're told, "At ABC Corp, our vision is to make the best widgets in the world, provide gold standard service to our customers, and to become the global leader in the widget industry."

The immediate following thought has to be, "As opposed to what? Making terrible widgets while providing second-rate service?" What exactly is "the global leader" and how will you know you're it? These bland, static statements tell your customers you lack depth, direction, and most of all, any reason to fully commit to a relationship with you.

On the opposite end of the vision statement spectrum, some pack themselves full of flowery language and lofty waffling. Consider Microsoft's vision statement, "At Microsoft, we work to help people and businesses throughout the world realize their full potential. This is our mission. Everything we do reflects this mission and the values that make it possible." It sounds great, but what does it mean? This could also be the vision statement of a company that makes office chairs, or publishes business books, or handles large conferences. Take out businesses and it could be about a gym or a church.

Or consider Avon's vision statement, "Avon's mission is focused on six core aspirations the company continually strives to achieve . . ." and then it goes on through another 249 words covering a variety of topics like surpassing competitors, increasing shareholder value, and fighting breast cancer. Comprehensive? Yes. But why in the world would a customer ever take the time to read it, much less care about it?

These types of statements, although pretty, fail to inspire customers by mistaking appealing language for actual depth.

Still other companies are unable to differentiate themselves from their competitors. Citigroup's vision statement is, "To be the most respected global financial services company. Like any other public company, we're obligated to deliver profits and growth to our shareholders. Of equal importance is to deliver those profits and generate growth responsibly."

You can't argue with that, but isn't that the vision of most financial service companies, or even most public companies at large? Why would a customer choose Citigroup or invest in its stock over its competitors? The same is true for small businesses as well. A local office supply store hangs their vision statement above their door, "You need it. We have it." What business couldn't use that as their motto? Even more, couldn't someone easily prove that statement was a lie by simply walking in and asking for a double cheeseburger with a side of fries? There are countless real-life examples from Fortune 500s to tech-startups mirroring this point almost exactly:

"It is our job to seamlessly develop functional, premium and maintainable growth strategies for 100% customer satisfaction."

"To be the providers of strategies and services, which deliver long term commercial benefits, based upon our clients key business requirements. The strategies evolved should be economical and efficient and allow the organizations to respond rapidly to both market and customer needs."

"We strive to develop a superior Internet browser for our users through state-of-the-art technology, innovation, leadership and partnerships."

"We promise to deliver high-quality technology solutions that enable companies to meet their business goals more effectively."

"Our vision is to be the best at identifying, qualifying and delivering software solutions and services that enhance our customer's bottom line."

Are you excited about engaging with the 5 companies above? Did you sense an emotional connection with the statements above? Were you inspired to join by those statements?

Not likely.

In truth, a vision statement is just a collection of nice-sounding words that never create connection with your customers and will never express the depth of who you really are. It's not that these companies are doing it wrong. The whole idea is anachronistic. They are leftover relics of a conventional brand development model that is either too bland or too overreaching, and fail to differentiate an organization in the real world. As such, it makes no sense at all to build your brand from a vision statement.

Compartmentalizing your story into a vision statement (or whatever you want to call it) systematically sterilizes the potential human connection out of your story and dulls the potential power it has to offer your audience. The result of a vision statement is over-processed, uninspiring, and predictable waste.

This may be breaking news to some, but **no one** cares about your vision statement. No one cares about your mission statement, brand promise statement, or whatever static statement the conventional model can manufacture. People are unable to connect to you in a vision statement. What people care about—and more importantly, what they connect with—is your story.

Stop writing vision statements, and start learning how to tell your story.

Free your story from the confines of structure and process to allow it room to breathe, to grow, and to become meaningful once again. No matter what your endeavor is, your story, not a static vision statement, is the foundational building block to forming relationships with your audience that deliver real value.

BURSTING THE FEATURE BUBBLE

Every startup's temptation is to build their startup story from their product features and benefits. After all, an intense amount of time goes into perfecting and implementing the feature mix of any product. But features are just one part of the overall value proposition. The problem with starting with your features is it places your story inside of a *feature bubble*. A feature bubble is an over-emphasis in talking about features not really justified by what will actually matter to your customers.

This is a natural way to think about your product, as features always seem more urgent and more concrete. If you build your story from just your features, you'll almost certainly miss the opportunity to get to the thing that really matters—the reason you built it in the first place.

Simon Sinek, author of *Start With Why*, proposed the idea of The Golden Circle contending great organizations create their foundation by first addressing WHY they exist, then HOW they go about doing what they do, and then finally, WHAT they do.[18]

From your customer's viewpoint, your WHY is the context in which products begin to make sense. In your customer's mind it's the WHY first, the product benefits (i.e. HOW the product benefits them) and features (WHAT creates the benefit) second. A product's features fulfill the promise you make to alleviate a pain (the functional-value promise). Your WHY tells your customers why the pain was worth alleviating, why you were the one to do it, and gives people a reason to care about you.

Your WHY represents the emotional impact your company has on an individual. It represents the journey that you and your customer undertake

to realize this emotional impact. A product can lead your customers to satis-faction, but your WHY leads your customers to being passionate about you. In a hyper-connected, information-rich marketplace, people are yearning to connect to something more than just a product with a specific feature set.

Your WHY as a founder results in your startup, and your startup's WHY results in your products, your brand, and your culture. In establish-ing your relationship with your audience, there may be no better question to ask yourself than, "Why do we exist?"

Maybe you exist to change the way people travel . . .

Maybe you exist because you believe in the power of connection and you want to make it accessible for everyone . . .

Maybe you exist because you want to get fresh drinking water to Zambia . . .

Maybe you exist to help children fall in love with music . . .

Maybe you exist to inspire people to make a change in their life . . .

Maybe you exist to help students graduate from college . . .

The truth is, you don't exist purely for money or profit. No company does. Nor do you exist purely for producing your products or services.

Profit and products are the results of your existence, not the reason for it.

To create value, you have to burst the feature bubble. Stop talking about how great your gadget or gizmo is, stop talking about the hundreds of clever features you've packed into it, even stop talking about how these features benefit people alone. Start talking about WHY you built it, start talking about WHY it matters, and start talking about WHY people should care about a relationship with you. Most startups can communicate

WHAT they do. Some go as far as to communicate HOW they do it. But very few excel at clearly communicating WHY they do it.

An entrepreneur we know was creating an iPad app that promised to get children to practice playing music more. We asked him what his WHY was.

"So kids will practice music more often, so the parents won't feel like they're wasting money paying for lessons."

But why are *you* committing your life to building this app?

"Because I'm a musician."

And?

"I want children to love music."

Right! And that's why the parents are paying for music lessons.

That the app will improve the practice routine is the functional utility. The aspiration that the kids will love music is WHY the startup exists and WHY the parents buy the product. Because the founder is a musician and understands the joy of music is WHY he committed to this particular business.

People simply don't connect deeply with WHAT you do or HOW you do it; they connect with WHY you do it. They engage with the WHY. They want to understand the WHY. They want to buy the WHY. If you can't clearly articulate your WHY, your customers aren't going to do it for you.

MOLDABLE SAND, PRODUCT FEATURES, AND COLLABORATION: BURSTING THE FEATURE BUBBLE

An Interview with Randy Apuzzo (Co-Founder & CEO) and Andy Fleming (Co-Founder & CTO)

Zesty.io was founded in 2010 in San Diego, CA, and plays a large role in the growing Southern California startup ecosystem. Both Randy Apuzzo, Co-Founder & CEO; and Andy Fleming, Co-Founder & CTO, have a wealth of knowledge and know-how in building products that work. Zesty.io, their flagship product, is tackling the content management and distribution space in a way that allows for collaboration between clients, designers, developers, content creators, and the many moving pieces across the Internet. Randy and Andy shared their Lean Brand story and talked about learning how to burst the feature bubble in their product development.

TLB: So first, people may not be familiar with you yet. Can you tell us what Zesty.io is?

Zesty is a cloud-based content platform. We originally created it to be able to make, edit, curate, and manage custom websites. It's evolved into an interface to collaborate, integrate, and distribute content to websites, social media, and applications. Ultimately, it puts the power in the designer's hands. They can design whatever they want and not worry about a client stepping in and creating issues.

TLB: Where did the idea come from and how did you start?

In the beginning, we built Zesty for ourselves and for our clients. We both, a long time ago, had our own agencies. Our agencies developed a lot of websites for a lot of clients, and in doing so, we both had a good sense of both the needs of the developer and the needs of the client in creating custom websites. We weren't happy with the way clients were sort of forced to use Wordpress, and more than that, we weren't happy when we had to fix whatever they broke. We were unhappy and our clients were unhappy with the tools that were available.

Out of that pain, we wanted to build something that could make our lives easier and our clients a lot happier. So we took on the challenge and built a system that we knew clients could easily use to edit their own content while we had full access to design whatever we wanted for them, and it worked. We didn't think about it being a platform for anyone else. Somewhere along the way we started realizing that other people could use it and we decided to try and make a business out of it and that's how Zesty, as a tech startup, was born.

TLB: Sounds like a big transition from an in-house tool to becoming a full-blown startup. Walk me through how that went.

Well, it's funny because we really stumbled and fell when we released Zesty for the first time to the public. We felt like we were doing all the "right" things to launch: we published it to Betalist, we threw a big launch party, we got coverage from tech blogs, and a bunch of other stuff. We got hundreds of users from all of this, and it felt great, but at the end of the day, it was all kind of fruitless.

TLB: Let me stop you there for a second. You launched with a bang, threw a huge party, got coverage in tech blogs, and ultimately got tons of users, but you feel like all of that was fruitless?

Yeah. It sounds crazy, I know, but it's true. It was like our features poisoned us.

TLB: What do you mean?

From the start, all we talked about were the features of Zesty, which meant that the only thing people could respond to and talk to us about were the features. Someone would say, "Well this other platform does this. Can your platform do that?" Or, "We really need this feature or that feature." Which lead us into this trap of just having conversations about this feature or that feature and then trying to develop our way out of it, which trapped us even more. From that point on, we were in a very dangerous cycle: the feature bubble.

It helps to know that our whole team (at the time) was made up of developers. Our company culture kind of revolved around developing. There was always something to develop and there was always some new feature to build. It became this feature-first mindset that sucked everyone into it. All we were focused on was just building more and more features, and at the end of the day, it was fruitless. It wasn't communicating. It wasn't creating any value for the people wanting to use it on the outside.

Looking back, you expect every feature you build to have big returns and it feels good to get one out. People may even use it, but it doesn't win any wars. It doesn't speak to people. Someone may say, "That is a cool feature," but nobody feels like it changes their world. Even the best feature we've ever released, it has never, ever hit people that hard.

TLB: That's a powerful insight and realization. Tell me about how you got yourselves out of it and what caused the shift.

At the time, we had hit some major milestones in our product development. Andy had completed this awesome cloud-based infrastructure, our development interface was good, our code was kicking, and our websites had some of the fastest loading times on Google. We had a well working, viable product. I (Randy) came in one day and said, "We are going to stop building Zesty." It was a big day and you could definitely feel the tension in the team because our company culture was built around developing and I was asking them to stop and slow down. You could feel everyone wanting to keep pushing, keep pushing, and keep pushing—next version of Zesty, then the next version of Zesty. Back then, it was kind of a crazy thought, but the idea was to stop building and start getting out there and talking to people about it.

TLB: Which meant branding?

Yeah. From a product standpoint, I think we built all the right tools; but from the brand standpoint, we found out that we had no idea what we were doing. We knew branding was important, but ironically we looked at branding almost like features. In a functional way, we designed beautiful elements (logos, colors, ads, postcards, and so on). We thought, if we had the right features in both the product and in the brand, that it was enough to convince people to buy it. But having a brand these days is much more than that. You just can't cut through the noise with a beautiful design or a feature rich product and expect it to be meaningful and create value for people.

Which is when we started our Lean Brand journey. We really struggled to switch from that feature-first mindset that poisoned our brains in the beginning and to start talking about where people connected with us, how we created emotional-value, and to get to the heart of our story. When we started making that shift towards lean branding, we didn't really understand the emotional language and how that ties into the product. The more and more we worked with it, the more we were able to start speaking that language and understand it. It's still tough for us to separate ourselves from the features of our product, but we now know the importance of it and are working on it everyday.

TLB: Tell me more about that transition and what you did to work through that major shift in your thinking.

We went through a lot of different challenges in that transition. We did a lot of exercises and a lot of working through the concepts together and trying to really understand how to connect with our audience.

One simple exercise we went through was actually one of the hardest. We had to describe Zesty without mentioning a feature or a function. It sounds simple, but it was challenging. It was just too easy for us to say, "Well, there's this feature, then there's this feature, and this one." It's tough when you are so close to your product and so invested in it to think differently about it. Talking about how our product connected to others and how it may help them in their aspirations was really challenging to process and to learn, but it made a huge difference.

Another exercise we did, one of the best ones, was the mall exercise. We each got twenty bucks and set off into the mall for 20 minutes to find one item that we thought best represented how people would connect with Zesty. We both came back with very functional items—a puzzle game and a canister of this moldable sand. When we talked through it, we realized that the puzzle and the sand both represented the functionality of Zesty—that you could build anything you wanted with it—and didn't represent anything about what that functionality may mean to our audience or how our audience could connect to it. That exercise really opened our eyes to how we approached talking about Zesty and helped us through that transition. Actually, we both keep those items as reminders on our desk.

TLB: Moldable sand? That sounds fun. How has breaking that feature bubble and applying Lean Brand principles transformed your organization? Has it helped you connect with your audience?

The biggest impact has been in how we approach our audience. We realized that it is not just our story or our product, but that we are a part of the story and our customers are another part of the story. We had to understand that there are multiple stories out there and you have to discover the commonalities and what is shared in those stories to really connect with your audience. We are much more confident in how we approach our audience now and it's working.

For example, we learned that the story around Zesty is really about collaboration. And that story has to be true in a few ways: it has to be true of your product, it has to be true in how you talk about it, and then it also has to connect with people. We had to really reevaluate our startup by asking ourselves, "Which features really communicate collaboration? What could we say or do to get someone to light up about collaboration? What aligns with that story?" We had to focus on creating real value with both our product and our brand to really break that feature bubble and connect in a powerful way with our customers.

TLB: Is it working?

Absolutely. It has been a lot more successful than just saying we have this feature or that feature even if we are talking about the same exact functionality. When you can put it in the context of how it impacts your customer's life or how it helps them accomplish their goals, or WHY you built it, it's a hundred times more successful than just talking about the feature itself.

You can't argue with purpose. They can't say, "That's not why you built it." Well, how do they know? We have an impression of how we think it will work for them and they have their impression of how well they think we did with it. But the point is that it's something that connects with them, and then the rest falls in line. We feel like we are really good at making products. But even if we were bad at it, if we could connect with people and then figure out how to make those features, it could still work.

We've learned so much more by building a relationship with our audience than we ever have with any product or idea. Now we are focused on getting a reaction from people and helping people really engage with us and what we're doing.

It's all a part of that complete story. There is the product itself but then there is how you relate with a customer and how they relate to you. It might be meeting them in person, or it might be support, or chat, or email, or any number of things. That story has to be consistent and it has to tie in together to allow people to experience you in a way that stretches beyond the functions of your product or even your product itself.

YOUR RALLY POINT

Working from your WHY, you can begin to shape your story around a common place where the pieces of who you are as an organization, who you are as a founder, and who your audience is can coalesce. Think about this space as a *rally point*. Your rally point represents the reason for people to gather around you and to join you "in the journey." It will represent your 'side' and also dictate everything else that doesn't fit to be on the other 'side.'

Organizations should have a reason to exist. No matter how great your product is, how successful your track record has been, or how much (or how little) money you have in the bank, people need a reason to get behind you. Give them a reason. Give them the depth they are looking for. Give them a common point to unite around and you'll create the potential for strong, long-lasting, and value-based relationships.

Underneath every great story is a rally point that people can grasp and latch on to. Ahab set out to kill Moby Dick, the legendary great white whale who took his leg, because he sees the whale as the embodiment of evil, and we root for him. Gatsby purchased his house, threw extravagant parties, and acquired wealth in the hopes of proving his worth to Daisy, and we identify with him deeply. Jean Valjean journeys through a number of reincarnations to redeem his old moral depravity, and we celebrate his transformation.

A startup must form solid ideas around what kind of imprint they want to leave on the world, use that to establish their rally point, and begin to operate from it. If you can't communicate WHY someone should join you; there are no reasons for your customers to understand where you're going, what you do, and how you are going to get there. This isn't about a short and easy path to selling a product, it's about inspiring an audience to believe in you enough to join you on the journey toward fulfilling your shared aspirations. You're either selling or you're inspiring. That's it. Stop selling, start inspiring.

To inspire, you must take a stand.

Your startup isn't for everybody and your market isn't an enthusiastic "Everyone!" The reality is, your startup is going to grow with a specific group of people who get who you are, understand you deeply, and identify with what you stand for. Although products may exist that are for everyone, they are few and far between and didn't start that way. Understanding who is most passionate about you and what you stand for is the key to creating traction for your startup.

You must work to build trust over time with this group of people by consistently adding value to ongoing conversations, establishing your rally point, and creating a depth of relationship your customers can only get from you. People are looking for organizations that have a point of view, organizations with an opinion, not just a specific product, promotion, or price.

For disruptive startups, where the market is unknown and the value is unknown, your rally point is the product. The product forms the cornerstone of the story because people are now able to do something that before they couldn't. This new product enables them to become something greater than before. For sustaining startups, where the market is known and the value isn't, your rally point is your point of view. What you're fighting for. What you're fighting against. What your unique line in the sand really is. This provides an avenue to engage your audience's aspirations through some emotional impact competing organizations lack.

Your rally point acts as a beacon for people to understand who you are and get behind you—or not. Just like relationships between individuals, groups, or even romantic relationships, shared aspirations are important.

If your shared aspirations are inconsequential, so is the relationship. On the other hand, shared aspirations that are considered important serve as the basis for strong friendships, marriages, groups, and brands.

So, what do you believe? What is it guiding you intrinsically forward? What do you stand for?

Start by asking yourself two simple questions:

1) *What are you fighting against?*
2) *What are you fighting for?*

Close your eyes and imagine a flag flying high on the side of the high-way. When a passerby drives past that flag, what does it stand for in their minds? What should immediately come to mind? What will they think about you? What will they feel about you?

If you stand for nothing, you will almost certainly fail to develop strong relationships with your audience. Stand for something, and stand by it. If you're a musician fighting to help kids fall in love with music, stand by it. If you're designers fighting to help people get in touch with their artistic side, stand by it. If you're an action sports junkie fighting to help other people tell their story through video, stand by it. Identify and define your rally point unapologetically. Place it front and center and allow it to impact your audience. This is how you can build a following of passionate people around who you are and why you matter.

FOCUS, FOCUS, AND REFOCUS

Once you can articulate your rally point, the biggest advantage you have as a startup comes down to one word—**focus**. Startups are unique because they have the ability to capture the imaginations, hearts, and minds of people through the simplicity of the story they tell. Lyft stands against inefficient and impolite taxis and for feeling like a world-traveler while making connections with locals. Square stands against rip-off bankers with expensive and complicated payment equipment and stands for being a savvy, modern businessperson. AirBnB stands against expensive hotels and for the adventure of home sharing and feeling like a local. It doesn't take much effort to understand Lyft, Square, and AirBnB at all. Their stories are succinct, confident, and simple to understand.

Large enterprises spend millions of dollars a year attempting to artic-ulate who they are in simple and understandable terms. They're just too over-complicated to do it well, making the relationships with their customers easily unfocused, fractured, and dilute. A startup doesn't suffer from over-complication. Instead, a startup is able to tell a potent story declaring exactly who they are, why they matter, and why people should participate.

The greatest startups focus on being great at a very small number of things. If you are to succeed as a startup, you have to pick those few ideals where you want to absolutely excel and shoot for the stars on those while ignoring the rest.

Focus may be the most important word when it comes to brand development. Rarely do you risk focusing too much, but focusing too little. Focus your story. Make it mean something and make it matter. That's the advantage you have in building an enthusiastic, committed, and passionate, audience.

Never lose sight of your focus.

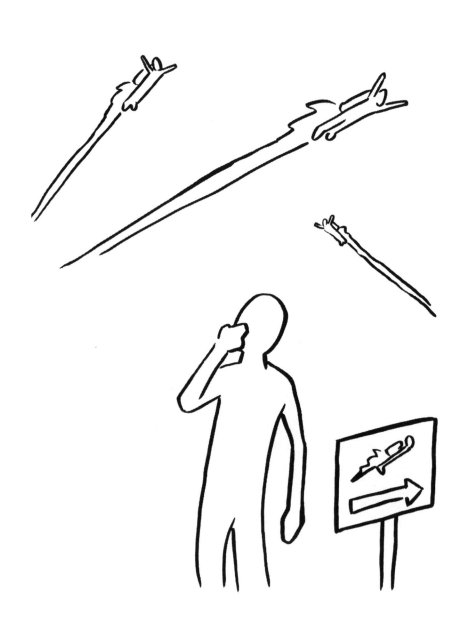

CHAPTER 6

ARTIFACTS

TRAILBLAZERS

The word "trailblazer" is often used in reference to iconic people like Amelia Earhart, Nikola Tesla, or Jackie Robinson—people who pushed beyond the common constraints of their times to forge new paths for generations to follow. But do you know where the idiom came from? While most of us may know the term best in its figurative sense, in the wilderness, a blaze is a type of marking that establishes a trail for other hikers.

While Earhart and Tesla were social and intellectual trailblazers, outdoor adventurers blaze their trails literally along the path they are hiking. The most common types of trail markings are paint blazes, which are symbols painted along the trail, or carved blazes, which are chiseled into trees or rocks on the side of a path. In the southeastern United States, there's even an old folktale of native residents tying rope to young treetops to make the wood bend as it grew, eventually creating a bent top that would guide the way to a village. No matter what form trail markings take, their ultimate goal is to communicate two basic pieces of information: where a hiker is currently, and where he needs to go next.

Just like a hiker marking his path, every organization leaves a trail. Whether intentionally or not, every symbol, image, paragraph, design, experience, advertisement, and so on an organization creates leaves a "blaze" that establishes a figurative trail leading their customers back to them. These types of symbols, expressions, and experiences are better understood as *brand artifacts*. The term *artifact* is very intentional here. Not only does the term recognize how people will find their way to you from a customer's point of view, it also recognizes the human nature by which we all relate to the world around us. As humans, we interpret the world through everyday interactions with our environment. We understand the outside world based on the relationship between sensory stimuli and our response to that stimulus. Over time, we create very specific responses and relationships to different types of stimuli.

We may cherish the smell of coffee in the morning, or love the feel of our favorite pair of jeans. We find comfort in the taste of a Thanksgiving meal, or hearing a song that "takes us back," or a photograph that "speaks" to us by merely glancing at it. Our sensitivity to sensory stimuli provides us with both knowledge and emotional connection to our environment.

These stimuli are *artifacts*.

The goal in building brand artifacts is to create a strong, distinct memory structure, by which your audience navigates a crowded marketplace to find its way to the value you are providing.

BRAND ARTIFACTS

On the continuum from cave paintings to social media updates, artifacts create an infinite palette of sensory expression that produces perceptual recognition and emotion, such as belonging, love, respect, loyalty, or advocacy. They provide information about the people, the culture, and the story behind them. They signal back to their creator and trigger varied responses that provide people with ways to engage with an organization, both emotionally and intellectually.

Brand artifacts are often part of the customer interface that was unin-
tentional or intangible. For instance, Chipotle's burrito assembly line,
Time Warner's lack of customer service phone numbers, the McDonald's
Dollar Menu, and the act of assembling Ikea furniture are all key brand
artifacts that aren't quite tangible and may have not been thought of as a
brand artifact. Artifacts can even be things that aren't necessarily a part of
the product or company itself like the lime that sits atop a Corona bottle
or the perfect amount of time to submerge your Oreo in a glass of milk.

At their heart, artifacts are **memory triggers**. Any cue (sight, sound,
touch, taste or smell) projecting your story and reflecting the relationship
between you and your audience is an artifact. When you think about them

in this way, artifacts are far more than an aesthetic veneer. They turn abstract meaning into evident cues, allowing consumers to better identify with who you are, your story, and ultimately what value you offer to them.

Artifacts are often the first things your audience sees or hears when they come in contact with your organization, whether it's your name, a symbol, or an experience. Ultimately you want these first interactions to prompt a customer to recognize you and distinguish your organization from another. But a successful brand is rarely about artifacts alone. Artifacts simply help your audience identify your company, shape expectations, and leave lasting impressions.

To that end, artifacts work both individually and collectively. A company's name, an experience, or an iconic shape or package can trigger a tangible association between the organization and the artifact. Collectively they form a recognizable memory structure helping to reinforce the relationship a customer has with an organization.

Every day we identify organizations from one another based on their artifacts. A curvy glass bottle with a red and white label evokes a relationship with Coca-Cola; a green tractor with John Deere; black and silver uniforms with the Oakland Raiders. In a world of complex symbolism, where symbols with deep cultural roots are modified, editorialized, and juxtaposed to create ever-new meaning, artifacts serve as a way for your audience to interpret the uniqueness of your organization and strengthen their relationship with you.

WHERE TO START (HYPOTHESIS DRIVEN DEVELOPMENT)

Although today you have almost limitless options when it comes to creating artifacts, there is a large difference between effective artifacts and artifacts that simply create waste. A lot of mediocre brands are that way because they spend too much time and energy creating a bunch of artifacts without understanding what their audience actually engages with. You don't want to turn into a generic brand with a veritable closet full of artifacts that never connect.

Most startups are far from the need of creating artifacts that might help connect them to as many people as possible. They are simply trying to create any connection at all. They must first learn the value they are providing and with whom. In the past year, we have been offered dozens of t-shirts from startups that are pre-audience, pre-validation, pre-Product-Market-Brand fit, and even pre-launch. If your startup is printing swag before you validate your relationship, you are not a startup; you're a t-shirt company.

So when it comes to brand artifacts, the most pivotal question a startup needs to ask is, "What do we think is the one crucial memory structure we need to establish with early adopters?" In other words, what is the minimum set of artifacts required so that our early adopters will connect with the value we've brought to them?

To answer that question, you must be actively engaged in learning.

Hypothesis-driven artifact development means having measurements in place to validate or invalidate the value of a specific artifact, within the context of where you are as a startup. The most effective artifacts should enhance your audience's understanding of your startup while having an emotional impact.

Your artifacts are likely to change, evolve, and mature over time. Don't give in to the temptation to fall in love with a particular artifact like your name, or your color scheme. Almost every Fortune 100 Company has been through a redesign, reboot, or complete overhaul of their brand artifacts at one time or another. Moreover, startups often rebrand when they achieve Product-Market-Brand fit, because only at that time do they truly understand their relationship with their audience.

You also don't have to choose just one version of an artifact to test. You can test multiple versions to discover what is most effective in helping form your relationship with your audience. As you learn what works, you'll be able to invest, scale, and build effectively without creating a lot of waste.

Hypothesis-driven artifact development is in stark contrast to what most brand agencies and geniuses offer. The conventional branding model is intensely focused on generating artifacts en masse. Agencies refer to these artifacts as "deliverables" and charge premiums for packages ranging from logos to full-blown "identity systems."

Waste doesn't happen just with startups. In a now infamous stumble, Pepsi invested over $1 million on a logo redesign by a top agency. In a 27-page document titled, "BREATHTAKING Design Strategy," the agency laid out justification after justification trying to prove that its logo was a veritable Da Vinci Code of artifact design, drawing on magnetic fields, Feng shui, the Renaissance, the Möbius Strip, the Mona Lisa, and the "Golden Ratio."[19]

The result? A slightly rotated version of the old logo with the wavy white line in the middle moving diagonally. Their audience's reaction? Pepsi's was heavily criticized in popular magazines, Internet forums, blogs, and the like not only for the ridiculous design strategy document and the outrageous cost of the redesign, but also because it looked strikingly like the Obama campaign logo. The "Breathtaking" redesign was anything but. In the conventional model, companies spend outrageous amounts of money "improving" their artifacts with only vague ideas, completely subjective opinions, and doublespeak.

At least Pepsi could afford such a debacle. For a startup, this could be a business-killing approach, costing a startup precious time, resources, and what little cash they might have.

The truth is, as a startup founder, you *don't know* which artifacts you need and which you don't, which will be effective and which will not, or which artifacts are crucial to building a memory structure and which will be ineffective. As long as you don't *know* the value you're creating and for whom, based on *transactions in the marketplace,* how could you know how to represent that value?

The only way to find out is to test in the market.

In many cases—like the Ikea and Time Warner Cable examples— the artifacts that work may not be the most obvious and are therefore unpredictable and unknowable to you at an early stage. Just because you want something to become a brand artifact, doesn't mean it will be. AOL founder Steve Case never could have predicted just how iconic the, "You've Got Mail," sound bite would become for the first generation of Internet users, much less that it would be borrowed to make a Hollywood blockbuster starring Tom Hanks and Meg Ryan.

Smart startups work to discover which artifacts create value by incorporating artifact testing into the DNA of their organizations. Test print runs, doodling, lo-fi prototyping, split testing, and multivariate testing can all help a startup to discover the value of a particular artifact.

Artifacts will only have meaning—and resulting value for your organization—when they are tested and shared with your audience, preferably in context with your product's value. Keith Ferrazzi, in his book *Who's Got Your Back* writes, "emotion, empathy, and cooperation are critical to success at a time when technology and human interaction are intersecting in new ways. Trust and conversation are crucial in this new economy."[20]

βetabrand

ZEPPELINS, FASHION SHOWS, AND DISCO JACKETS: ARTIFACTS THAT TELL A STORY

An Interview With Chris Lindland (Co-Founder & CEO)

It's true; one of the favorite pieces of clothing I own is a Blue Velvet Reversible Smoking Jacket. And where do you go to get an amazing smoking jacket complete with a skull button? Betabrand, of course! Betabrand is an anything-but-ordinary clothing company known for their unique voice, amazing clothes, and for mashing up finer fabrics with fun, surprising designs (think pinstriped hoodies). They have developed a passionate and devoted audience (which they lovingly refer to as "Model Citizens") around their startup. Chris Lindland, founder of Betabrand, talks about how they learned to create artifacts that inspired people to join the party.

TLB: What's the Betabrand story? Where did this all come from?

So there are two stories. There's the predecessor to the Betabrand story and then there's the Betabrand story. The predecessor was called Cordarounds. I had no investors prior to starting Cordarounds and the business had shown itself well enough that I would get investors coming to me wanting to invest in the business. I decided I wanted to change the name of the company so I could be more general and people wouldn't just be asking if our pants were made out of corduroy. So that's where Betabrand came from. The theory behind Betabrand was it was a name where reinvention was a daily event. The most defensible part of it is the name itself because I knew we could always change it. I made sure we were open enough and willing enough to be able to experiment along the way. It didn't take a ton of time to come up with the name, Betabrand. It didn't take a ton of time to create the logo. But it took a ton of time to develop what that meant.

TLB: You're in a pretty dense (sustaining) space in the retail clothing industry and people have some pretty strong connections with the clothes they choose to wear. Tell me about being a startup in that world and trying to develop a story that is divergent from the rest of the stories in your category.

It's a big challenge to go into the clothing world and say we are going to create aspirational clothing because then you are going to be fighting with the budget of Ralph Lauren. Or to say we're going to create aspirational athletic clothing, then you are fighting against the talent and brand and identity of Nike. Those are pretty mighty competitors out there for people to connect with what you're doing. We sort of said Betabrand is going to be about creativity and experience. There are not a lot of brands telling you to be creative.

Instead, they are sort of saying, "live your life," or, "be your-self," and stuff like that. We were just saying, "be creative." We figured as long as our voice was creative enough, people would allow us into their own personal conversation of what it meant to be creative.

For us, it wasn't making a statement that, "we are creative." Instead, we were engaged in the act of being creative and engaged in the act of trying to find interesting things to do. I think it's easier to try to present yourself in this sort of ivory tower of creativity, but Betabrand will never be that. Who we are enables us to, in turn, make a clothing statement. We are able to earn the right to participate in people's concepts of what it is to be creative.

TLB: That's a great concept—earning the right to participate in your customer's story. How did you go about creating artifacts that projected that story and earned you the right to participate with your audience?

We have a model of 99% fiction 1% fashion. We purposely have foul language and humor in our newsletters and it's about exploration. From the beginning, we told the story of boundless ambition. You know, an evil multinational corporation has to start somewhere.

We had this ninety-nine year plan to build a pan-shaped zeppelin floating over the city of San Francisco and there was never any doubt that it was going to happen. It will just take ninety-nine years and so I wouldn't even be alive when that finally happened. We would do job postings for jobs ninety-nine years from now and stuff like that. We found out there was this guy that was going to Antarctica with a pair of our pants, so we claimed Antarctica in the name of Betabrand. Then we started lobbying for the existence of Greenland to be declared a continent so that we can be popular there as well. These stories had this conceit. It's huge and everybody had to accept the inevitability of it all. Ambition was a big part of the story.

We also did a lot of events. We always wanted to be "the world's first" to everything, and so hyperbole was something that always helped. For example, we put on San Francisco's "First Certified Single Male Fashion Show" every nine months and it was always called "the first" every time it happened. It didn't matter. Hundreds of people would show up because everyone knew it was just a joke. They would be able to go out on stage and be a star and they always came out committed customers thereafter because we gave them an experience. In reality, they were just the most low budget fashion shows of all time. I mean a keg, period, and nothing else.

And we would report on the phenomenon happening in the world of our fans. 80% of the stories were fabricated but 20% were real. That was the editorial point of view that we took. Hyperbole became the basis of the greater part of the business and the relationships really evolved from that point of view.

TLB: Can I get a ticket to the Zeppelin?

Sure . . . when it's ready.

TLB: You balance this ambitious, grandiose vision with a really playful and hyperbolic tone. Where did that style come from?

Betabrand's writing style is unique in the clothing business but not unprecedented. There's a writer named J. Peterman who ran a clothing brand driven by stories and sketches. It was a catalogue business back in the 80s and 90s and he even became a Seinfeld character. In terms of what we are doing within our industry, we still pale in comparison to what J. Peterman achieved in storytelling. We're more humorous, but I would feel like I was discrediting the amazing achievement of that brand by proclaiming that we are the best storytellers of a clothing brand.

It is also based on me believing, long ago, that if *The Onion* sold clothing, it would be the greatest online retailer ever. So we ask ourselves, "Are we as good as *The Onion*?" Only on the best, best, best, best, best day have we put together a newsletter that reads as well. So I don't expect *The Onion* to become a retailer, but man I can't tell you what guy wouldn't love it if they had a clothing brand as well. Credit where credit's due, there are great, great writers out there and we are just trying to do what we can with the products we have and the ideas we have.

TLB: And it's working. Why do you think people connect with your story and why do they get behind you?

In the beginning, it was a celebration of smallness and candid spirit and ambition that won us a lot of followers at that time. It was just an honest recognition of where we were, and where we wanted to go was something that was so beyond impossible, it didn't make anyone feel like we were thinking we were larger than life. We were very clearly incredibly small, but people appreciated an enthusiastic and hyperbolic vision of being successful. There's a very positive, inclusive tone in speaking about a Zeppelin large enough for ninety-nine workers plus livestock. We are always reaching the point of being obnoxiously ambitious to then bring it back to joking around.

The way I think about it is there are more aspirational screenwriters out there than there are successful screenwriters. Successful screenwriters can afford to buy Gucci and Prada, but everyone else can't. We provide the clothing for that lifestyle of struggle and creativity. That's the way I would approach it because it made it seem like I was talking to people that I knew and that I love. I've always known people who are actively trying to succeed creatively and I know who they are, I know what motivates them, and I know it's fun to talk to them. So if I imagine those will be the people we'll be speaking with, they can come in different shapes and sizes and forms, but there is a sameness among those people.

TLB: Coming from that perspective, what types of artifacts have you found work to engage those people?

If you give your audience a platform from which to tell the story and you make sure they feel their effort is deeply rewarded for being the star, they really connect with you. So our general point of view is that photos are better when it's someone else's photo.

Playing around with our logo, we discovered that a "B" turned to the side looks like a really stupid pair of sunglasses. We said, "Wow! That's like putting a moustache on a photo. What if we get people to take a photo of them with these dumb glasses on their faces and give them a discount if they did?" And the answer is: thousands have. We call them our "Model Citizens" and they are featured on our website and in our social media accounts and so on. It makes me laugh every time because it's so stupid looking but it's pleasantly stupid and funny.

We use the tools we have available to advertise, like our newsletter, Facebook, and Twitter. These are very big culture building connections and very good opportunities to connect with our audience. We get a lot of people to participate and we get to see the images and see all the stories that way.

What we hope is that certain communities will own certain parts of Betabrand where they will drive product development and present the product as it should be experienced and do a lot of the work in that way.

We are editors, for sure, because some photos are better than others. But what's happening with it and how it got roots in different communities around the world is because we invite them in. For example, the way our disco stuff is taking off right now. We didn't do anything to make that happen, people just started sending us ideas and photos and we followed. We don't want to play cop with our audience; we want to see what they are doing on their own, how they express it, and what they do about it.

TLB: What tells you when it's working and when it isn't?

Open rate and click rate. If we choose this editorial path and it delivers better open rates than the rest of the industry, we've got to be doing something right. And if you were to read a newsletter from Betabrand you'd say, distinctly, that it's jokes and it's funny photos. If the numbers are there, then awesome. It's also fun to build up an audience that way because you get to play with lots of fun stories and lots of fun photos. Then you can add all of those things to your website and add to that creative perspective.

The premise of a venture-funded company is that either you succeed or you don't. Right? And I hope we did. If along the way we ended up creating a great brand, then awesome. The real test will be whether we make it. Which is to say, if crowdsourcing and crowdfunding and crowd photography and really great interactions with customers really can create a good monster revenue generating business, then good for us. But we are deeply invested in all those things. And we know we look like what we all imagine the modern brand should look like; whether that is a big financial success only time will tell.

We are doing well right now. We keep getting lots of customers and we've been successful, but we don't know how things will change two years from now. We don't know if we will become hackney because there's a lot of other brands that are trying to look like Betabrand. And where will we go?

TLB: Change your name?

Right. That's a joke I've always wondered about. If we were a titanic success, I would love to buy the domain brand.com and then take the "Beta" out of Betabrand. It will be hilarious to act as if that was the plan all along, right? But I would assume that domain brand.com is a million dollar plus.

TLB: More than likely. That'd be really funny though.

I would never pay that for one joke that I love, but it'd be great.

TLB: Betabrand seems very comfortable in its story. A lot of startups struggle to find their story and really articulate it. Why has this worked so well and what advice do you have for others just getting started on this journey?

I would imagine it would suck for some people to read this and be like, "Well it's just two of us, and we are doing it on our own credit cards right now." Believe it or not, back when I ran the company on my own credit card it was the same thing. When people look at Betabrand today, they can't say, "My God, I'm never going to catch up to fourteen thousand images and all these stories and all these committed customers and all these products." From a brand development point of view, it has always been the same story for us; it's just a lot bigger now.

I had to work harder in the beginning when the audience was just a handful of people, but it has always been the same consistent story.

I think we first had to be an admirable creative voice in our own right. Then people wanted to play ball with us. For example, we don't go out and search for people to collaborate with us because they are famous. We want famous people to come and want to collaborate with us. I've always rejected any offer to be part of some Hollywood gift bag just because some celebrity is going to get my stuff. My attitude is, truthfully, f*** that. They have way more money than I have and they can go shopping in my store, so I am not going to do that.

What I've learned is if you have a voice that is truly your own, and you seem comfortable with that voice, then people who have far bigger followings than you or are actually famous, want to collaborate with you because they want to work with other creative people. For instance, Stephen

Colbert keeps buying our stuff. We are nowhere near as talented as anyone on his staff, but we also seem—well, comparing to a titan in humor like that, it's unfair to make any comparison—but we try. And I think the effort is rewarded because people who are in the creative business come to us to collaborate. We've got scientists and famous chefs and these types of people, but the first thing they want to do is work with us and the next thing they want to do is figure out if there's money in it for them.

You have to achieve that voice before people want to play along with you. We can now speak in lofty terms with these famous people, but it was just a lot of regular people we had to convince first. If you can't convince a regular person to play along with you, you're never going to get a famous person. You've got to make sure you have a zillion regular people first. I think a lot of people think they can jump ahead, and that's wrong. If you're good, and you're creative, and you're interesting and someone out of your league sees you, even famous people can become customers.

You have to have your own followers and your own audience. To build that, you have to talk all the time about your story. For us, we are asking things like, "Is there a crunchier way of telling stories? Is there a more inquisitive road that we should take?" These are really good questions to ask.

EFFECTIVE ARTIFACTS PROJECT, REFLECT, AND BUILD

As you develop your artifacts, be sure to stay out of the weeds. Focus on "high altitude" attributes that are magnetic to your customer and your team. Big, emotional ideas—not product features and benefits—are at the heart of the best, most enduring startup artifacts. The product produces utility value, the brand represents the emotional value, in other words the impact the product and company in total bring to the customer.

Early on, you want your tests to have reasonable fidelity, but you shouldn't have to pay exorbitantly. Once the lo-fi prototyping of the artifacts are validated in the market, you can invest more.

It's much less wasteful to nail the validation of your story first, and then invest in the projection of the relationship through artifacts down the line.

Effective artifacts share a few things in common. They:

1) Project who you are.

2) Reflect the relationship you have (or want to have) with your audience.

3) Build an instantly recognizable memory structure over time.

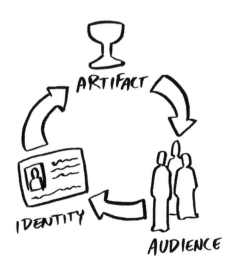

In a Lean Brand, you want to discover, through experimentation and validated learning, which artifacts create the most traction in building the relationship you desire with your audience. Your vehicle for learning is your MVB. Every organization must iterate on the right mix of the most effective artifacts that engage their audience with the utility and emotional-value it provides.

WHAT ABOUT MY LOGO?

Talking about artifacts may cause you to instantly start thinking about a logo. By now we understand that branding is more than just a logo. Still, many entrepreneurs' initial instinct will be to start with a logo. They spend precious time, resources, and money in an effort to create their logo and then plaster it in as many places as they can think of from business cards to the back window of their car. It may look nice, be well designed, and even feel great to have, but in all reality, their logo didn't get them one step closer to building a meaningful relationship with their audience.

Let's be clear about what a logo actually is. A logo, short for logotype, is business jargon for a trademark made of custom-lettered words that, together, form an identifying mark to signal a business entity. Typically when people say logo, what they are really referring to is a trademark. That's why the ™ is used when a company is claiming trademark rights but the logo is not officially registered (the ®—for registered—is for those trademarks actually registered with the United States Patent and Trademark office for those in the US).

There are different types of trademarks used to identify a business entity. A trademark can be a symbol, icon, monogram, badge, sign, or other graphic device. Shell uses a symbol, whereas LG uses a monogram, for example. Logos have been around in one form or another for several thousands of years. The Ancient Egyptians branded domestic animals with hieroglyphs to signify their owners. The Romans and Greeks marked their pottery with identifying marks to identify their hand.

By medieval times, the use of marks was commonplace and even became required for certain goods. Guilds began to form for groups of skilled laborers from stonemasons to brewers and their marks helped to protect their goods against inferior offerings. Nobility began using heraldic marks to identify their status and property and to signify their armies on the battlefield that were called coats of arms.

At the start of the twentieth century, with the introduction of color printing and the birth of advertising, trademarks tended to use a mix of national, nautical, heraldic, and agricultural illustrations. The public generally understood these symbols and the meaning behind them. Nautical and agricultural illustrations represented purity and freshness whereas heraldic illustrations, like crowns and lions, represented dignity and status. The "Modernist" movement in the 50s and 60s began to simplify the illustrative form down to their essence with marks like IBM, AT&T, UPS, and John Deere.

Despite a rich history and what conventional branding "best practices" may teach, starting your brand artifacts with a logo is a waste. Why? Very few people, if any, see a logo and immediately decide it is so remarkable, so incredible, and so significant that they can't help but share it with their friends and can't help but engage with the organization that created it. Why would they? There really isn't anything remarkable, distinguishing, or even necessarily unique about a logo. Flip through any logo book published by Taschen and you'll see dozens of logo designs blending together in a sea of unrecognizable organizations.

In the short run, and especially when you're in the initial stages of establishing your relationship with your customers, a logo probably is the most limited expression of that relationship you can possibly create. This is because the point of your brand development is to develop a relationship with an audience based on shared value. Put simply, designing a logo that doesn't reflect the relationship you end up discovering creates waste.

If you aren't convinced yet, here are a few more reasons why you don't need to spend much time and resources on a logo:

- A logo is one-dimensional.
- A logo has a short shelf-life.
- In use, a logo is typically pretty small. (Average size on a website is 150px x 30px)
- A logo isn't really unique. Every startup has one.
- Most of all, a logo is not remarkable. No matter how great your design is or how clever it turns out, the chances of it creating value on its own is slim to none.

In most startups, there are few "must have" artifacts, if any. A company name will suffice as the logo; a tagline is fine, once company value has been validated in the marketplace. Worrying about a color palette is superfluous. The 1000s of "how to name your company" articles are bogus. Cisco, Yahoo, Google, and Facebook didn't win because of logo, company name, or tagline. Neither did those doom Pet.com, Webvan, or Friendster.

In an overflowing market crammed full of companies, everyone is trying to make a mark. The organizations that win are those who make a mark by creating engagement and interaction, not by trying to stand out by designing a logo. Nike made the swoosh, the swoosh didn't make Nike.

DYNAMIC NOT STATIC

Most artifacts are static, meaning, they are one-dimensional, fixed, and passive expressions of your brand. Logos, color schemes, billboards, and

TV commercials are all static. Countless startups spend their entire marketing budgets on the creation of things that live in a one-dimensional world. Although some of these artifacts can create small amounts of traction, for the most part, they only serve as weak expressions of a much larger story. The opportunity, and challenge, is to focus your efforts around the creation of *dynamic* artifacts.

Dynamic artifacts are interactive, energizing, and magnetic expressions of your brand that invite your customers to engage with your story, your value offering, and your startup rather than observe them. The best dynamic artifacts take into account all five of our senses. Dynamic artifacts can create expressions of your brand that are immersive and irresistible.

Martin Lindstrom, in his book *Brand Sense*, called this moving your brand from "2-D to 5-D." Lindstrom wrote, "Bonding with a brand, like bonding with people, requires a multi-sensory experience. The more sensory touch points you can leverage, the more powerful the bonding memories will be. That's why it's important to consider every possible sense to ensure a systematic integration of experience. This will stimulate the imagination, enhance your product, and bond your consumers to your brand. The first step in creating a sensory brand is to provide a stimulus that can be attached to your brand and your brand alone."[21]

Rainn Wilson's startup, SoulPancake (which we'll talk directly with in Chapter 10), demonstrated the difference between static artifacts and dynamic artifacts with an expression in Venice Beach called "Heart Attack."[22] In the artifact, a mysterious, large white box placed on the busy Venice Boardwalk was positioned with a simple button that read "Need some love? Push here."

When a passersby worked up the courage to press the button, the box exploded open with streamers and smoke and a troop of people dressed in red and white with heart boxes on their heads came dancing out of the box. Much to the button-pusher's delight, they encircled them, tossed confetti, and administered hugs all in an effort to express the notion that "everybody needs love in their lives, but sometimes it can be hard to find." The faces of both the button-pusher and the collecting crowd were filled with joy, adulation, and delight at the unexpected experience they were given for pushing the mysterious button.

What an incredible way to tell a story and invite people to join their rally point. What makes this artifact remarkable is it engages the story SoulPancake is telling in a dynamic way. Even more, it creates an amazingly remarkable experience for the people there that day and for people who are lucky enough to see the video.

With some creativity and a willingness to take some risks, your options are limitless when it comes to expressing your story through the use of your artifacts. Don't worry about the longevity of these artifacts, worry about the remark-ability of them.

What if, instead of spending the money on a logo or a fancy landing page, a startup who designed an application to make financial saving more simplistic, decided to host an experience where they put people in a money machine and allowed them to take as much money as they could grab in 30 seconds. Don't you think the money machine would create a lot more traction and enthusiasm for the application, for saving money, and ultimately for the startup, than a logo?

Or, what if instead of spending the money on getting letterhead printed to send out "official correspondence," a startup who was trying to change the way people make friends, decided to stick a ball pit in the middle of a Boston sidewalk with a sign hanging over it saying, "Take a seat, Make a friend." And then encouraged people to meet complete strangers to share

a conversation together. Doesn't is seem the ball pit would create a lot more traction than the letterhead?

Between a logo and pub crawl, which one do you think goes further in building a relationship with your customers? (If your answer to that was the logo, perhaps you've never been on a pub crawl.)

Although these types of artifacts may be misconstrued as PR stunts, they represent something much larger than a stunt. They represent capturing opportunities to tell your story in ways that engage and delight your audience. PR stunts are about you, dynamic artifacts are about your customers. What would a dynamic expression of your story look like? Chances are, it would be pretty amazing. Moreover, people would engage a lot more with that expression than they ever would with a nicely designed logo.

In a startup, where budgets are limited and attention is scarce, dynamic artifacts should always be preferred over static artifacts.

PUTTING YOUR DUCKS IN A ROW

Every time your customers experience your brand, it should feel familiar. Whether they are using a product, talking to a service rep, or making a purchase from their iPhone, the interaction should feel cohesive, recognizable, and comfortable.

All your artifact choices need to grow out of what you've learned—and decided—about who you are and why that matters to your audience. Your approach to artifacts should never devolve into "I like (or don't like) this photograph or that photograph." Save those discussions for when you're decorating your house. Rather, make choices to help your audience see you as you really are and want to participate in your story.

Developing and/or renovating artifacts for relational connection is more like weaving together a mosaic than it is carving a sculpture out of a single piece of stone. You'll place some of the tiles, others will place some, and some will place themselves. This "artifact mosaic" requires a different toolbox than the one used by conventional branding practitioners—one based more on shared thinking and co-creation and less around rules and guidelines. Artifacts, in this way, allow you to iterate and evolve as your business changes and grows.

Which one artifact do you hypothesize will relate who you are and why you matter to your audience in the strongest possible way? How can you tell your story dynamically? Which artifacts do you think can give you an instantly recognizable memory structure with your audience? Choose your artifacts with intention and care. Build from places you've learned create traction and don't invest in anything that doesn't.

CHAPTER 7

INVITATION

THE FIELD OF DREAMS FALLACY

Despite being one of Kevin Costner's most memorable movies, *Field of Dreams* captures an emblematic motto pervasive throughout the startup world, "If you build it . . . they will come."

In real life, the "Field of Dreams Fallacy" plays itself out in beliefs evident throughout the startup community.

"If we build a better X, people won't be able to stop themselves from buying it."

"If we add feature X, then people will finally buy our product."

"If we have better X, then people will come."

"If we change our messaging to X, then people will come."

"If we just say Y, then people will finally get it!"

What's closer to the truth is, "if you build it, they won't come." Just because the app is built, or the business plan is written, or your marketing strategy is in place, does not mean customers will come and keep on coming.

Julien Smith, author of *Trust Agents*, aptly noted, "You already know this intuitively. There's a reason people don't join your groups, subscribe to your mailing list, or share your content. It's why they're not telling friends about your business. It's also why, in the long run, you will become the vultures and hyenas of the attention ecosystem. Effective immediately, the reality of the new world is that if you build it, they won't give a shit."[24]

How are you supposed to create traction around your product? How can you get to your first thousand—or million—audience members? Starting from zero, it feels impossible. The answer isn't to get more marketing glitter, hire a PR firm, or push ever-shallower messaging. Putting marketing glitter on a product doesn't inherently make a product more valuable; it just makes it shimmer.

The answer isn't in adding more features either. The startup graveyard is full of feature-rich products dead and buried before they ever found traction in the marketplace. You must build a product people need. Without validating the need, you're sunk. But just building a product isn't enough. To avoid the startup graveyard, you must form a strong relationship with people and allow them to become passionate about who you are, what you built, and why you matter.

When it comes to the relationship, what's lacking is deftness in inviting people to the party. The startups that succeed are those who turn their app, SaaS, service, gizmo, gadget, or whatever they've made into a compelling invitation for customers to join them on a shared journey of value creation.

The better motto is, "As you build it, invite, invite, invite!"

INVITE, INVITE, INVITE

Invitations are active calls for people to join you as participants on a shared journey of value creation. It's much more than "messaging." What you say, where you say it, and how you say it impacts the way people respond to you. There is no tricky language or marketing-speak here. Although, on face, inviting someone to join you is a simple concept, there's a lot to creating invitations that work. To start with, there's an attention deficit. People are feature-rich, information-rich, and attention-poor.

A few years ago, the *Washington Post* decided to run a social experiment about attention. They enlisted the help of musician Joshua Bell, one of the world's finest violinists, to play in a busy metro station in Washington DC on a January morning during rush hour. Completely incognito in street clothes, Bell played some of the most intricate pieces of music ever written with a violin worth more than $3.5 million dollars. Out of the thousands of people who passed by in the 45 minutes he played, only 6 people stopped and paid attention. When he was done, no one noticed, no one applauded, and no one gave any recognition to his performance.

The *Washington Post* experiment, quite literally, showed a microcosm of just how real our attention deficit is. The journalist behind the experiment, Gene Weingarten (who was awarded the Pulitzer Prize for the article) wrote, "We're busy. Americans have been busy, as a people, since at least 1831, when a young French sociologist named Alexis de Tocqueville visited the States and found himself impressed, bemused and slightly dismayed at the degree to which people were driven, to the exclusion of everything else, by hard work and the accumulation of wealth. Not much has changed."[25]

Not much has changed, indeed. In 2013, we each sent over 30 text messages a day[26], cumulatively watched more than 6 billion hours of video per month on YouTube[27], spent more than 2 billion minutes a day on Skype[28], watched over 1000 hours of television per month[29], sent over 144.8 billion emails worldwide a day[30], and each spent over 11.2[31] hours per week reading those emails. We are certainly attention-poor.

The sheer amount of marketing messages today is stifling. Fifty years ago there were, perhaps, three major communication mediums: radio, television, and print. Back then, people would give you their attention if you simply asked for it. You'd interrupt their TV program with a commercial, and they'd listen to what you had to say. You'd put an ad in *Time Magazine*, and they'd look at. You'd sponsor a radio show, and people would listen.

That's not the case anymore. Reliable statistics on advertising are hard to come by, but rough estimates of the amount of marketing messages we see in a day range from about 300 all the way to 20,000.[32, 33, 34] Even on the low end of the spectrum, it's a suffocating amount. Our brains can't possibly process, notice, and absorb, much less judge the merit of 300 messages a day, let alone 20,000. All this to say, we live our lives bombarded by messaging.

To complicate things further, there is no indication this trend will disappear anytime soon. Re-targeting campaigns are getting more extensive, the Connected TV advertising horizon is growing, the addressable TV possibilities (sending a specific TV commercial to an individual household) are being realized, and with the introduction of new Bluetooth low energy (BLE), and the ensuing use cases BLE implies (as demonstrated by Apple's iBeacon), it won't be long before marketing messages become micro-targeted literally throughout every aspect of our daily lives.

It is getting harder and harder every day to gain people's attention. For a startup, where failure to connect with an audience ensures an expedient trip to the graveyard, how do you invite people to join you? How do you create relational traction? How do you win advocates? How do you develop an audience?

In lean thinking there's a concept called *pull*. Pull refers to an arrangement in which nothing is done in product creation or delivery until the customer (including internal customers in the design and manufacturing process) expresses a need or demand for the product or for the intermediate "deliverable" from the downstream process. Put simply, pull means

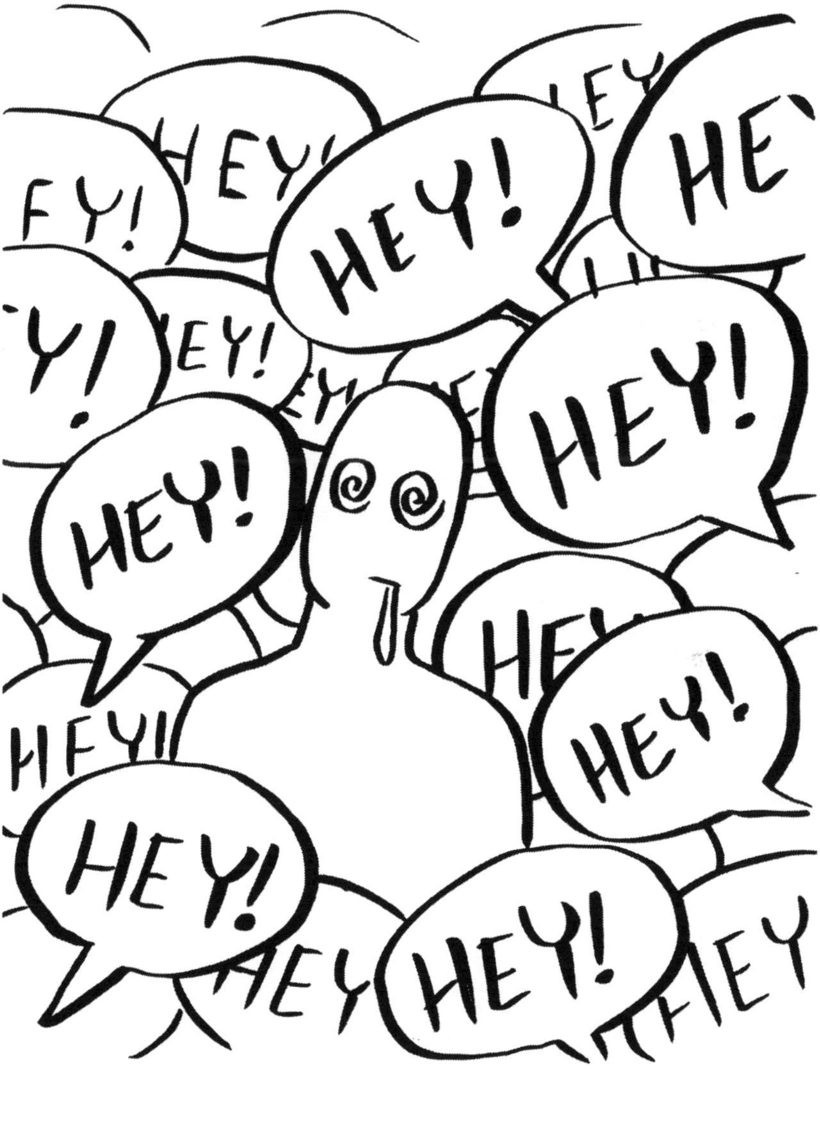
HEY!
HEY!
HEY!
HEY!
HEY!
HEY!
HEY

not doing anything until there is demonstrated demand. Don't roast the beans, grind them up, heat the water, brew the coffee, or pour the cup until the coffee is ordered.

In Lean Branding, we can apply the concept of pull to our invitations. *Message Pull* is the work of constructing invitations based on validated demand generated from a customer. No activity in the stream of invitation creation is executed until we can demonstrate a real demand for that activity.

To use message pull successfully, you must know who your audience is, create content (messaging) based on the pull (demonstrated demand) of that audience, and figure out the best medium in which to talk to them.

YOUR GUEST LIST

Ask any first-time entrepreneur who they plan on selling their product to, and the most likely answer will be, "Everyone!" The nets are cast wide in expectation to catch all the fish in the sea and copious amounts of capital are exhausted trying to ensure the brand has mass appeal. Lean branding goes the opposite way. To be successful, you must start by focusing on who you believe will be most passionate about their relationship with you. Great organizations understand they can't be all things to all people.

The words "target market" may immediately enter your mind when you start thinking about who your audience may be. Push them out as quickly as you can and never let them return! Talking about customers as "target markets" quickly dehumanizes and de-values your potential relationships with customers. Understand your market is composed of real, living, breathing, feeling people. They aren't targets, demographics, or data. Targets, demographics, and data don't buy your product, people do. Terminology matters because it forms the basis for how you relate to your customers. Instead, think about your audience in terms of real people, or *personas*.

Personas

Personas are archetypal sketches of the type of people who you hypothesize will interact with your organization. Although they can be profiles of fictional characters or rough outlines of people based on ethnographic research, surveys, interviews, and intentional customer development; it's actually best to use a real, living, breathing person. If you don't, the urge to create stereotypes can be too strong. Even large design firms fail to create replicas of real people because of their overuse of surveys and statistics based research. Why not just go find the real person? Personas illuminate descriptions of real customers who share similar behavioral patterns, purchasing preferences, use of technology or products, lifestyle choices, and the like.

Put simply, a persona is a real, fake, or potential customer painted in real-life dimensions.

Personas go beyond simple demographic or psychographic data. Demographics are temptingly easy to collect and enticingly self-organizing, but do little to give you a comprehensive view of your customers. Demographics are about what (age, race, income); personas are about why (behaviors, preferences, attitudes, motivations). To develop relevant personas, don't focus on people's surface "likes" and "dislikes," but instead focus on who they are, what they do, what frustrates them, and what delights them. Their behaviors, attitudes, and motivations are key to finding insights about the people you believe will be most passionate about their relationship with you.

One small caveat about personas: the idea of building models of your customers, what they need, and how they differ from your competitor's customers will be most beneficial if you've already reduced their profile down to people who are already purchasing products in your category—especially if you tend toward the sustaining side of the innovation spectrum. If you intend to open an organic burrito truck, for example, you can create multiple thorough personas for your customers, but you're wasting time unless you've already sorted them out of the existing groups of people who eat out at burrito places, eat out at organic places, or go to food trucks.

A great persona will take the shape of a narrative and describes a person's typical day, their experiences, struggles, wins, hopes, dreams, skills, attitudes, associations, background, and environment, complete with photos, props, and other relevant pieces of information to get a holistic view of your audience. Details are important. Vague descriptions are unhelpful as they typically lead to broad generalizations and diluted insights about potential customers. You need detail to color in the lines of your persona's sketch. Be as detailed as you can without allowing the exercise to become superfluous.

Here are a few example persona questions to get you thinking:

What is his or her name?

Where does she live? In an apartment or in a house? Does she rent or does she own?

What keeps them up at night?

What's his favorite fast food restaurant? Fine dining? Pub?

What kind of car does she drive? Did she buy it new, or used? Dealer or resale lot?

Who are his friends? What are they into? What do they do together?

Who worries them?

How do they perceive themselves?

Where does he hang out after work? What about the weekends?

Favorite sports team? Athlete? Olympic event?

What do they aspire to be?

(In Chapter 12, we've developed a tool called the *Persona Grid*. When you begin your persona work, you can use this tool to help you sort through the details of creating useful personas.)

A COHORT OF ONE, A COHORT OF MANY, MANY COHORTS

Once you have your core personas sketched, you can begin the work of segmenting them into groups based on various sets of value criteria. Ben Blank from Intuit talks about segmentation in terms of *cohorts*. A cohort is a group of passionate people advocating and supporting the growth of your startup. Facebook built its empire from a cohort of college students demanding to be invited to join and only permitted to do so once their school or university was "accepted" into the Facebook platform. Fashion startups like Trunk Club, Huckberry, and Frank & Oak are building their relationships around the demand of a specific cohort of men who are diving into what's being called "The Art of Manliness." Cohorts give you a way to understand what your customers actually demand.

Often startups focus too much on trying to gain masses of users from the start. Before you can worry about 1000 users, you have to be able to find your first one, first. Start by forming a *cohort of one*. Can you convince one person (who isn't your mother or college roommate) to become passionate about you? Will one person engage with you and what you have to say? Can you get one person to join your story?

If you can form a cohort of one, you can use what you learned from that one to focus on growing your audience into a *cohort of many*. This segment is centered around the group of people you believe will be most passionate about their relationship with you and who would look to one another to recommend companies and products they become passionate about. As a startup, you need to learn how to create relationships with a core, narrow, well understood, and well-defined segment of people who share a pain, passion, or preference.

When you've nailed down the delivery of value to this narrow segment, you're set up to start scaling to grow your audience into *many cohorts*. There are many ways to grow your audience (which we will talk more about in Chapter 10). You may choose to use "bowling pin" strategy by knocking down new markets based on their similarity to your primary market, or you may expand into new territories and geographies, or you may choose to grow your product and line extensions to further your reach. No matter how you grow, with each cohort you are building from what you've learned rather than guessing at what you think may work.

Cohorts are not exclusively about money. People have potential value beyond just cash. Influence, adoption, longevity, ease of reach, depth of pain, the size of the market, and values are also criterion to take into consideration when working out your market segments.

Like most things in life, there's no one right way to do segmentation. You cannot understand the relationship forming with a particular cohort, however, without diving deep. You may prefer to choose one segment at a time, dive deep, and then move on to the next if the first one fails. Or you may prefer to go less deep across multiple segments until one becomes the leading candidate. The goal is to know and understand your audience

COHORT OF ONE

COHORT OF MANY

MANY COHORTS

deeply. If you don't understand your audience, you will never be able to measure the message pull demanded by the people who are passionate about you.

BROADCAST VS. INTERACTIVE

Ultimately, the relationship you form with your audience will be co-shaped, co-defined, and given meaning by your audience. Remember, a brand begins to take on meaning when there is synchronicity between who you are and who your audience wants to become. Their perceptions about you, your value, and your relationship with them matter deeply to how you go about building and iterating your invitation. As in any relationship, both what you say and how people receive it matter.

Conventional brand development was built around linear, one-way messages delivered through one of three mediums—TV, radio, or print.

An organization would develop a message to be broadcast to the masses. This form of messaging has long been the standard operating paradigm for conventional branding practitioners. But today, communication is a dialogue. People have the ability (and are using it more and more) to respond directly back to any sender of any message. This shift has put the company and the customer on equal footing.

To demonstrate the shift, imagine a hypothetical room full of about 100 people in Portland. Imagine these 100 people, within a few moments of one another, tweeted out a message reading something like:

"The @Target in San Diego is falling apart! The aisles are filthy and the staff is nowhere to be found . . . #gross #fail #shame."

What do you think the impact of those tweets would be? Do you think someone from corporate headquarters at Target would be on the phone to the manager at the San Diego location? Even more, wouldn't you think someone's job might be immediately on the line? And yet, all the people in Portland were lying! They weren't anywhere near San Diego, much less inside of a dilapidated Target.

One-way broadcasts, assuming complete command and control, no longer work. People are too savvy and communication is too interactive to rely on a broadcast. To be relevant in today's context, you must go beyond a broadcast and become interactive in the way you connect with your audience. To connect in a powerful way, you must learn *what to say*, *how to say it*, and discover *where best you'll be heard*.

sharethrough

NATIVE ADVERTISING: LEARNING HOW TO CREATE VALUABLE INVITATIONS

An Interview With Rob Fan (Co-founder & CEO)

Sharethrough is a leading voice in the "meaningful content movement" and is helping organizations create more meaningful content through their in-feed advertising exchange. As the world gets more and more digital, the gap between audience and organization is widening. Rob Fan, Co-Founder of Sharethrough, talks about their journey, the concept of native advertising, and weighs in on learning how to listen to your audience.

TLB: What is Sharethrough?

We've built our platform with the idea of trying to find or figure out a way to monetize the modern Internet with all different types of meaningful content out there. So in a simplified way, what we do is essentially take the advertising platforms that exist on Facebook and Twitter—from feeds to stories to tweets—and we give the rest of the Internet that same platform to plug into their sites.

From the publisher's perspective, they think of us as a way to monetize their feeds; and they have tons of feeds now. Everything is newsfeed driven, but they have no way to monetize other than decorating it with banners. So we provide them with a way to monetize their feed directly in the same way that Facebook is monetizing their feed and Twitter is monetizing their feed. Advertisers come to us as a way to get their content in very relevant, highly placed locations.

TLB: Tell me a little more about when you started. Tell me about that journey.

We started as a Facebook application company. That was a quite a while ago. But we started by building these little viral apps knowing that they weren't actually what the business was going to turn into. What we were looking for was trying to understand the new mediums that exist out there and really trying to figure out what the best new way to monetize the Internet essentially was.

We saw that advertising on the Internet was broken and needed to be changed. So that's when we started dabbling, trying to figure out how to change it and trying to figure out the right words to describe what we were trying to do.

Then the term *native advertising* is something that we came upon about a year and a half ago; maybe even two years now, where we heard Fred Wilson say it in a podcast or in some speech and we just resonated with it. That was the exact way we were trying to describe the kind of advertising we were dealing with and the places where this advertising goes. We ran with the idea.

TLB: Native advertising is analogous to figuring out where to show up and what to say (invitations in the TLB Framework). You have your fingers on the pulse of a shifting landscape in terms of advertising and how the world is connecting there. Tell me a little bit about why native advertising is a better approach than the conventional approach.

I'm not the first person to be saying it, but the Internet has shifted the role of the organization or anyone that has a message. You just can't force feed messages down individual's throats now. You have to be giving someone something first before they're willing to accept what you have to say. People's intolerance of being force fed messages has risen so high that as soon as they hear somewhat of a sales pitch, or somewhat of a blatant ad, they just walk away and ignore it.

The thinking behind native advertising is that you're providing some piece of content, something that's funny, that's entertaining, that's informational, that's a how-to, something that provides value to the person that is reading it. So when you do present them with your sales message, whether it's a blatant pitch at the bottom sponsored by your company, or a subtle mention, the consumer isn't immediately ignoring you. It's interpreted as, "Wow, they've given me something really valuable," so now I'm willing to give back in some way or create some space in my mind for what they have to say.

I think that's the major reason why native advertising is impacting the landscape because there's so many choices, so many ways to consume content now. If you aren't creating content in a native way, you're pretty much just trying to advertise and most people will ignore it. Or you get a really bad reputation because you're known as being really annoying and that you don't want to give anything in return.

TLB: So what should you be focused on when creating invitations that don't sell but give value to the customer? What are some of the ways you're seeing this done successfully?

At Sharethrough, what we do in terms of invitations is to create infographics, white papers, different kinds of bylines, and blog posts. None of them are a blatant Sharethrough ad, but I'll talk about Sharethrough and directionally point to the way Sharethrough can help you get your content distributed across the Internet.

I really think it's all about the value you're creating. So even if you're going to pump out a blog post a week, make sure those blog posts are valuable. If they're not valuable and all you're doing is saying a random statement and then advertising for your company, it's worthless.

You could go to the extreme where you don't advertise at all, but then you're also not living in the reality of the world where advertising does drive a lot of interesting things in the world. So I think in a world where advertising does have to exist, there must be better ways to do it.

That's the biggest reason why native ads have become so important is because people can read bullshit so easily nowadays. People can react like, "ugh, that's not really a true statement," or, "I don't believe you." Immediately you have some distrust and you have to prove yourself rather than a customer saying, "I'm on your side. I totally get you." I think that's why you need to be very genuine with the messages that are going out because people can easily tell if it's fake or if you're just trying to sell.

TLB: How do you figure out the difference between those two— selling and providing value? How do you gain learnings and measure to figure that out?

It's interesting because what you are dealing with is trying to make decisions based on what your gut feeling says versus the data. The way I view user feedback and data is that it comes in two forms—qualitatively or quantitatively. In quantitative data sometimes you can get data fully opposed to what your gut feeling is saying and you have to call into question is the data even correct? Did I come up with the right metrics and so on?

But when you deal with qualitative data, there is still data being generated in hearing, "so and so said x fact." Well, how many other people said x fact? Then that fact must be true versus just the bias the person has. We can then factor that piece of data into what we want to build.

There really is a meshing of the two. Where you want the company to go and what the data is telling you the company should be doing is a tricky balance. You always have to wonder am I asking the right questions to gather the data. That is true whether it's a quantitative number or it's qualitative feedback because you could ask leading questions, you could be looking at the wrong metrics, you could misreading, or misrepresenting the data.

I think it's important to do it many times and collect data in different ways because then you'll start to see more clearly. The fallacy in qualitative data is that someone could say, "yes, that's great, that's great, that's great" but they never buy it.

I don't think there's any easy answer other than when it doesn't match up to keep challenging the hypothesis because you may not be asking the right questions or you yourself may not be seeing the right questions.

TLB: What advice would you have, looking back, to other start-ups about building relationships with their audience? Now you clearly know who your audience is and have had success on both sides of the coin.

There's unfortunately no such thing where you come up with one wonderful message and then you're done. You have to iterate on your message. You have to try it out, pitch it. In the same way as if you're honing your elevator pitch, you need to hone your elevator pitch to your customers. That applies to your marketing message. That applies to branding invitations. Once you start to figure that out, then you can double down on it.

You know, the trick is not to do the expensive branding and marketing activities on a test message. I feel like a lot of startups fall prey to that mistake. They say, "Yes! This is it! Let's do it!" And they'll double down on the product or create that one blog post to try and get PR. One of the things we learned early on is PR is used only to increase your funnel and you don't do PR unless you're ready to increase your funnel. So if you're pre-launch, with nothing for people to buy, why do you need press? Maybe for hiring but there are probably other ways to do it because you're essentially pigeonholing you and your company without giving you any room to pivot or to iterate or to learn.

We really had a lean approach to understanding what our customers want and positioning and packaging that in the right way. We had to be willing to trial and error our way through discovering what they actually wanted. We started asking really basic things that we should have known if we were already established in the space, but we'd never done it before so we just simply asked. That gets you about fifty percent of the way and then past that was really just having conversations. A lot of our learnings have come from having interactions and that's how we're able to adjust how we invite clients to join us and what we're building.

WHAT YOU SAY

Recall, message pull tells us a startup should only create content once they can demonstrate the demand for that content and have clear ways to measure the success of the invitation they create.

There is no doubt content marketing is the new darling of the marketing world. The Internet is packed full of "top 10 lists" of content marketing best practices and templates for quick and easy content creation. Companies, both big and small, have bought into the concept of content marketing. Although content marketing may be necessary in an established relationship, it really doesn't have a lot to do with inviting people to join your story. In a startup context, where time and budget are scare, generating vast amounts of daily content can be costly, time consuming, and can quickly become unsustainable. Generating content for content's sake is unproductive to establishing a cohort of passionate advocates for your organization.

That's why using the tight measure of message pull is extremely useful when it comes to *what* you say. So many people make the mistake of looking at what others are doing and copying it. That's a good way to look competent, but not compelling.

When Mint got its start, they did a remarkable job of using message pull. Mint looked at the existing market and discovered an underserved cohort in the personal finance realm—young professionals. Through experimentation and validation, they quickly learned what type of content was being demanded from this segment of people and then delivered that content through an effective medium, a blog.

Jason Putorti, the founding designer at Mint, described the thinking behind their strategy, "quite simply we focused on building out a unique personal finance blog that spoke to a young professional crowd that we felt was being neglected." Eventually the blog became the highest read blog

in personal finance and worked to drive traffic to the Mint app. The app itself didn't have a high viral coefficient but their content did.

Before you start generating content, you have to first understand what content to generate. Let's take a hypothetical example of a SaaS (Software as a Service) startup offering a better way to manage your Pez dispenser collection.

The starting point for discovering the message pull would be the personas created in the initial customer development. What are our customer's lives like? Where do they shop? What corollaries can we find? Let's say what we found was people who are passionate about Pez dispensers were also passionate about retro toys as well. Perfect! Why not test the demand for content based on nostalgic toys? We could tell the story of the Rock 'Em Sock 'Em Robots, write odes to the toys we loved as a child and still have, and explore the origins of the Cabbage Patch Kids. This type of content can deliver value far beyond the product itself. But the key is not just in the content, but in the journey you're inviting your customers to join you on.

Through experimentation and measurement, if we learn our content has demand, then we continue to produce our content. If we learn there is no demand, then we can go back to our personas and frame another experiment.

HOW YOU SAY IT

What you say is about understanding the message pull of your content. *How* you say it is about generously sharing your knowledge, insights, and soul—in the context of your rallying point—so people are drawn to engage with you over time. It's about the rally point your story is articulating and the strength of that articulation. The most powerful and compelling way to do this is also one of the simplest: *be you.* Be true to the story you're telling and to your unique voice. How you say it comes down to a simple structure: story first, value second, and style third.

Story First

Remember Chapter 5? Your story is the foundation for the message you want to send about your organization. Start with your story. Tell people who you are as a founder, what you stand for as a startup, and share your point of view. (Think: What is the one thing my startup stands for no one else can replicate? What's our rallying point? What is our aspiration?) This isn't a call to plaster your "about us" on every type of message you write. Instead, it's about sharing your story in multiple ways, shapes, and forms while being consistent with the point of view you're communicating.

Legendary baseball announcer Vin Scully is highly regarded as the best announcer in professional sports. His philosophy is based on this simple principle of storytelling, "Statistics are used much like a drunk uses a lamppost: for support, not illumination. If I can get a story about a player, I would give you a ship load of numbers, batting averages and all just for that one precious story." To create invitations that compel people to listen, break out of the "about us" box, and start painting a picture for the audience you want to talk to.

Value Second

You must articulate why you matter. (Think: "What do they want? Why should my customers believe what I am telling them? What do they aspire to gain from us?) Amidst the noise of all the competing claims your audience is hearing, why should they believe what you are claiming? The truth is, you can never have enough "reasons to believe." Think about this in terms of the reward a customer gets for interacting with you.

Threadless, the phenomenally successful T-shirt company with millions of tees sold since their founding in 2000, puts out dozens of new products a month—with no advertising, no professional designers, no sales force, and no retail distribution. And they're extremely successful. That's because Threadless has done a great job of articulating why they matter—participation. Threadless has told this story time and time again to their audience and has structured their entire organizational voice from the participation perspective.

Jake Nickell, Threadless co-founder, explained his approach saying, "I started Threadless as a hobby—a project that could be a creative outlet for design professionals to make something fun in their spare time. The first iteration was simply a thread on the Dreamless forum asking people to post designs in the thread and promising to make the best ones."

Threadless has created a powerful relationship with artists because they get to see their art printed on t-shirts and worn out in the real world, along with a small financial reward for winning the contest (initially this was only $100). Threadless has a powerful relationship with their customers because they get to participate in the manufacturing process, be exposed to some pretty fantastic art, and support artists. Both the artists and the customers have clear "reasons to believe" in Threadless.

Startups who understand why they matter, what value they will deliver to their customers, and can communicate it clearly without hesitation, are able to stand out in a sea of messaging noise. To stand out, what you say must be about the value being created for the customer. It's comprised of the functional-value of the product, plus the emotional-value of your brand. This is the aspiration, the hope you have around the impact of the product. The invitation is the messaging that tells your audience about this value and convinces them to give the relationship a try.

Style Third

Style is the way you end up articulating your value to your market segments. These are the actual words, phrases, headlines, and taglines you'll employ in creating invitations. It's helpful to start by narrowing the limited but powerful set of obvious, direct and highly-meaningful key message pillars—no more than three—your relevant audience is most likely to respond to. (Think: What's in it for them? How can we say it best?)

YunoJuno, a startup bringing together great designers (UX, graphic, developers) and innovative companies, has nailed a tone of voice in their messaging. They're funny, quirky, unconventional, and just a bit off kilter . . . and it's working for them. Co-founder Shib Mathew describes it this way, "Yes it may be different but more importantly—it's us being ourselves. The three of us are a pretty easy-going bunch. I'm an Aussie so it's dispensed at birth like Pez. Chris and Hugo are jaded enough fellas as well so a Monty-Python-esque approach to life simply becomes a vocational asset. We're serious about making a difference but if we weren't true to ourselves, YunoJuno and its community wouldn't get the most out of us."

Obviously having a copywriter on the team can help, but it's not a pre-requisite for successful invitations. Becoming a better writer is more about effort and practice than it is about an MFA in literature. Focus on the personality of who you are as a startup, as a founder, as a team, as an organization, and what is authentic to the story you want to tell. What is your unique perspective? What is your unique voice? Customers don't often comment or complain about language, so you have to find out for yourself what works and what doesn't work; what's authentic and what's inauthentic. Your style should tell your story through the lens of your unique personality in a way that resonates with the intended persona.

WHERE YOU SAY IT

Just as important as the message being sent is the *medium* through which the dialogue takes place. A medium—like social media, television, or a website—influences how the message is perceived. Imagine if the same Target lie mentioned before used a medium like a printed letter or television ad. Would it have been as successful? Would it have had the same impact? Probably not. The use of Twitter was as important as the message we sent.

To illustrate further, let's compare a Hollywood film to a website as we know them today. It's possible to communicate the same general content in both media (plural for medium). But, because the media are inherently different, we experience the content in entirely dissimilar ways.

A film takes you through a linear experience with a beginning, middle, and end. Over the course of the movie, we watch the characters and story unfold working towards some sort of conclusion. Since the creation of film, this idea has been integral to the planning and development of a movie production. The decisions made about the production of the movie are all heavily influenced by the medium, regardless of what the message may be. *The Breakfast Club, Saving Private Ryan,* and *Anchorman* were all conceptualized with the medium of film in mind.

If you move the same content over to a website, the experience changes dramatically. In the context of a website, information is rarely presented to a user as a linear experience. Instead, characters, scenes, and plot points might all be split up into different pages, parts, or sections. The user then decides how to consume the information to reach a conclusion. The conceptualization of a story like *Saving Private Ryan* would be completely different in the medium of a website.

This thinking isn't new. Marshall McLuhan coined the phrase, "the medium is the message," back in 1964.[35] To be clear, McLuhan asserted a medium affects the audience not only by the content delivered over the medium, but also by the characteristics of the medium itself. McLuhan's famous phrase argues that the medium is as important as the content delivered through it.

But for a startup, it isn't enough to simply say, "The medium is the message." The farther your startup tends towards the right (disruptive) side of the innovation spectrum, the more important the medium you are communicating through becomes. The farther your startup tends to the left (sustaining) the more important the differentiation of your message becomes.

Both of these scenarios are best understood in the context of message pull. The medium through which your invitations are sent tells your audience what to expect. If you send a new message down an old path, you're likely to miss your audience. In the same way, if you send a message down

a dead path, you'll miss your audience completely. The task for any startup
is to decipher the medium most appropriate through which to connect to
your audience.

DISRUPTIVE PRODUCTS & DISRUPTIVE MEDIUMS

For disruptive products, how you get to the customers is as important,
if not more, than what you get to the customer. Existing mediums provide the wrong context for innovative products. The more innovative the
product, the higher the need is for innovative channels, contexts, and
mediums.

For product-centric brand development (disruptive) existing channels
and contexts won't work. That means you must find ways to manufacture
the context in which your invitations are sent and co-evolve them with
the growth of your organization.

Tesla Motors, a relative newcomer to the auto industry, is an amazing example of this principle. Despite not spending a dollar on traditional marketing activities, Tesla Motors has captured the minds of the
American public like very few companies, including Apple, have been
able to do. Walk into a Tesla retail location in a fashion mall and it's often
more crowded than the Apple Store, which is saying something, especially considering you can't even buy a Model S there. One explanation
for Tesla's boom can be attributed to the Innovation Diffusion Curve[36].
The curve argues that most innovations follow an S-Curve as they diffuse
through the market. Tesla's product offering (the electric car) seems to be
trending at the uptick in the curve.

The S-Curve is part of the answer, but it doesn't account for the way
Tesla is connecting with their audience. From a branding perspective, the
other piece of the equation is the medium. Instead of selling their Model
S or Model X in the existing auto industry context—the infamous "mile

of cars" car lot—Tesla manufactured a retail experience within an unrelated medium—the fashion mall—to connect its value offering with an audience. What's more, you can't buy a vehicle and "drive it off the lot" immediately. Instead, a few clicks on their website, a credit card deposit, and you're the proud owner of a new Model S.

If Tesla had come to market using existing mediums of established auto manufacturers, it's more than likely they wouldn't have been able to differentiate their message enough to withstand the advertising barrage of players like Ford and General Motors. To even establish a small foothold with an audience, they would have needed vast amounts of capital to compete with established competitors spending billions on traditional advertising a year in the existing medium. But, by manufacturing the

medium in which their electric vehicles are communicated and sold, Tesla has been able to create traction with an audience large enough to rely on word-of-mouth marketing as it ramps up sales.

The more disruptive your product is, the more you have to work at discovering and or developing the medium through which to deliver your messaging. Exponential growth is the result of delivering your invitation through an uncontested channel. To discover an uncontested channel, you must test often, fail quickly, and validate your best thinking around which medium to go for. Steal, copy, borrow, remix, plunder, ransack, and invent. Developing a medium that works is critical to developing a relevant audience.

SUSTAINING PRODUCT & DIFFERENTIATED INVITATIONS

For message-centric brand development (sustaining) this means deciphering which existing media to deliver your message through based on what you've learned about your customer. If you tend to the sustaining side, you have to be able to differentiate yourself within an existing market via messaging beyond your product features and benefits. The choice of media and channels becomes important in the differentiation of your message.

With the rise of the Internet came the rise of channel possibilities. Facebook, Twitter, LinkedIn, Buzzfeed, Reddit, delicious, Instagram, Picasa, Flickr, Pinterest, Google+, Yammer, Banjo, LivingSocial, Meetup, Vimeo, Feedly, paper.li, Klout, Eventbrite—you get the picture. And these are just a sampling of the online channels available. Add in additional channels like print, email, press releases, sales tactics, and internal communications, and the number of choices can be paralyzing.

Because of the vast number of channels available and the resulting frenetic pace to saturate them all with messages, there is an overwhelming emphasis on speed and quantity. Emphasizing speed and quantity comes at the expense of depth and differentiation. Instead of investing in producing original content to create real relationships with audiences, many organizations have become data collectors repurposing information under the sheer pressure to get a post delivered.

For a startup, this type of thinking results in a frenzied collection of channels and a resulting dilution of the potential strength of the overall message. Facebook post, check! Twitter post, check! Instagram post, check! Pinterest post, check! And on, and on, and on. Blanket messaging turns into white noise rather quickly.

Did you ever drink Kool-Aid as a kid? The rule with Kool-Aid is simple—the more and more water you add the less and less potent the sugary-sweet taste of Kool-Aid becomes. If you add too much water, The Kool-Aid Man's slogan quickly changes from, "Oh, Yeah!" to "Oh, No!" Messaging through every possible collected channel is like diluting your Kool-Aid, and no one likes watery Kool-Aid.

What's worse is that blanket messaging can create a phenomenal amount of waste within a startup's initial brand development activities. Post, post, tweet, repost, share, write, post again. Concentrating on speed and quantity are the wrong things to focus on in building relationships with real people. Sure, there are businesses that survive this way, but they walk a thin line between providing content and being spam. Nobody likes being spammed. To build the type of relationships you need to be successful, you shouldn't need to risk becoming spam.

More channels + more messages ≠ more customers.

Instead, a startup needs to discover the most effective channels and the strongest mediums in which to connect with their customers. This means before you develop a tweet strategy for Twitter or a pin strategy for Pinterest, you must validate (through experimentation) the influence of the specific channel you've chosen to reach your chosen audience. To be most effective, narrowing your channels down to one or two highly influential channels, where the demand for the content being delivered can be demonstrated, will create the most traction for a startup.

Validated channels + validated invitations = more customers.

If you're willing to put in the work up front of recruiting the right advocates through the right channels, you'll be able to discover the demand for your messaging in a relevant audience. If you can nail the medium, the rest of your brand development activities will flow much smoother and have a larger impact on the relationship you're developing from there.

TYING IT ALL TOGETHER

What you say, how you say it, and where you say it tells a lot about you to your audience. There is no "right answer" to inviting your customers to join you. You must experiment to find an effective mix of content, style, and channels to create a compelling reason for people to join you. Mahatma Gandhi got it right when he said, "Happiness is when what you think, what you say, and what you do are in harmony."

To learn what works, startups should run small-scale experiments to test your invitations from different angles in small and safe-to-fail ways. Using small, contained experimentation allows emergent possibilities to become more visible. The emphasis is not on ensuring success or avoiding failure, but in allowing ideas that are not useful to fail in small, contained, and tolerable ways. The invitations that work can then be adopted, amplified, and scaled.

Ultimately, your audience isn't going to be aware of all of the tough experiments, decisions, and choices you've made in creating your invitations. Instead, all they will see is the final product. The goal is to learn which ones work and which don't.

To that end, invitations are not a one-time activity but a steady practice. From pre-launch to exit, you'll need to continuously iterate and improve the way you invite people to join you. New mediums will emerge and new channels are sure to emerge with them. Old mediums will die, and so too will the channels they offered with them. Your options will invariably ebb and flow. The constant, then, must be your willingness to explore and validate which mediums and channels provide the best context to tell your story.

To build capable invitations for people to join you, reject the "Field of Dreams fallacy" and figure out how best to invite people to your party.

If you build it, and invite, invite, invite . . . they might just come.

PART III
MEASURE

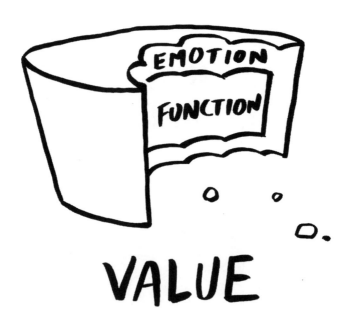

VALUE

CHAPTER 8

THE EMOTIONAL-VALUE STREAM

VALUE IS EVERYTHING

In the 1990s and 2000s, the main focus of executives was on creating wealth for shareholders. The absence of value for the customer in lieu of speculative wealth-creation led to vast fluctuations of the stock market and multiple historic crashes. The dotcom boom in the late 90s was proof of this. Small Internet firms like Boo.com, eToys.com, and Webvan were catapulted into the stock market stratosphere by wealth-focused investors' over-enthusiasm for their stocks. Ultimately the boom busted, leading to not only the liquidation of hundreds of these companies, but to the meltdown of the market itself.

Fast forward to 2007. Wealth-focused financial institutions and short-sighted lenders inflated the market to an $8 trillion housing bubble. The resulting loss of wealth, combined with the downturn in consumer spending and the financial market chaos, triggered the eventual bubble meltdown and ensuing recession.

Arguably both of the last major recessions, bubble meltdowns—whatever you'd like to call them—can be traced back to a reliance on short-sighted speculative incentives rewarding non-value creating activities in an attempt to increase short-term wealth: the *wealth-creation economy*.

As a result, the wealth-creation economy is in decline. On the heels of financial collapse, a new wave of value-creating organizations has emerged and is rapidly challenging legacy businesses, establishing new markets, and disrupting the entrenched wealth-creation mindset.

Value is everything.

In the new *value-creation economy*, if you fail to discover the value you hope to create in the marketplace, you'll never get off the starting blocks. This is true whether you are business to business (B2B), business to consumer (B2C), B2B2C or any other combination you might conjure up. This is true whether you offer a physical product, an app, software, hardware, a service, or even just an opinion column on a blog. To be successful in the value-creation economy you must discover the value you are creating and for whom that value is being created.

Lean Brand development is optimized for the discovery and formation of value. Value is not realized in brilliant assumptions, genius strategies, or creative ideas alone, but instead occurs where creative inspiration meets the rigor of validation. It's realized in the hard work of learning where actual customers connect with you and adjusting, iterating, and growing your brand to meet those connections.

WHAT IS VALUE?

From the 50,000-foot view, it's easy to use the term value as a ubiquitous, all encompassing term, devoid of real meaning. The first instinct is to think about money. A textbook definition of value would agree, "the amount of money that something is worth: the price or cost of something."[37] But to a customer, value is not just monetary. A customer perceives the value of a product or service in terms of their relationship to an organization, both in tangible and intangible terms.

Yes, people must decide whether a product is worth the sticker price. But with decisions about price, customers are making judgments (some subconscious) about the problem the product solves, the way they feel about the company who produced it, and the impact the purchase might have on them.

Which is to say: value is multi-dimensional.

Robert B. Woodruff, in his article, *Customer value: The next source for competitive advantage*, writes, "At a low level, customer value can be viewed as the attributes of a product that a customer perceives to receive value from. At a higher level, customer value can be viewed as the emotional payoff and achievement of a goal or desire. When customers derive value from a product, they derive value from the attributes of the product as well as from the attribute performance and the consequence of achieving desired goals from the use of the product."[38]

For any startup, and for all endeavors in business for that matter, recognizing the multi-dimensional nature of value is vital to your ability to create it.

There are two kinds of value: *functional-value* (the basic practical value a product offers as a category), and *emotional-value* (the emotive value customers believe they will receive from any product from your brand). Generally, products are responsible for creating functional-value through the tasks they accomplish. Brands, however, create emotional-value through the relationship they facilitate. All the activities a company does—resulting in its brand—are responsible for creating emotional-value for its audience.

That's why, in the context of Lean Brand development, **value** is defined as the **functional benefit** plus the **emotional impact** *as experienced by your* *audience* (the customer). Both are responsible for what a customer perceives your product or service to actually be worth.

FUNCTIONAL-VALUE

Functional-value describes the problem or pain your potential customers will "hire" your product to solve for them. This is a classic pain and solution framing of product development. A customer has a pain, a product is invented and developed to alleviate the pain, and if it is successful, functional-value is created.

Consider a product like Liquid Paper®. Prior to 1951, when Bette Nesmith Graham invented the first correction fluid using the blender in her kitchen[39], if you wanted to erase a mistake you made on paper your options were severely limited. You could cut it out, cross it out, or—much to the pain of many typists—simply start over again. The invention of Liquid Paper® provided a solution to a very specific pain. If you wanted to fix your mistake, you now had a product making it easy and efficient to do so.

It wouldn't have mattered if Bette had called Liquid Paper® "Pop Tarts," because it was the only product solving the pain for the customer. Although today, competitors like Wite-Out®, Tipp-Ex®, and even Boo Boo Goo® exist, the ease of fixing a mistake—the functional-value—is still the driving force behind the customer's perceived worth of Liquid Paper®.

Functional-value is about the task a customer is trying to accomplish and the utility of a product in accomplishing that task. In purely functional terms, if another product is introduced that solves the problem better, that product should win out. And yet we know from experience, that that isn't the case. Why is that?

EMOTIONAL-VALUE

Emotional-value describes the relational bias or preference we have for one product over another, and, more importantly, one company over another. Emotional-value is how your customers think about the unique relationship, attributes, and expectations your organization has to offer that no one else does. People form sets of expectations and partiality about purchasing from one company over another based on the emotional relationship they have with that company.

Take, for example, a Louis Vuitton handbag. The functional-value of a handbag is simple: you put your things in it and carry them around with you. There are many products a person can "hire" to solve this pain. A plastic bag from the supermarket, a canvas bag from Trader Joe's, and a North Face backpack can all carry items from one place to another with relatively the same ease. More to the point, a generic handbag purchased from any big-box retailer accomplishes this task just the same. The functional-value of all of these solutions is, for the most part, equal. Additionally, one can expect the Vuitton bag to be made of high quality materials and have a stylish appearance. These go beyond utility, but still represent product "features."

But a Louis Vuitton handbag costs upwards of $1000, whereas a generic bag costs around $30. What's the difference? Certainly the quality and appearance in themselves don't warrant such a markup.

People who purchase a Louis Vuitton handbag receive the recognition of those in the know (luxury conscious and possibly hip-hop friendly fans) that they shop Louis Vuitton. They're sending a specific signal about what they can afford, their taste, and so on. But all upscale makers offer quality and prestige. Is there something more?

What makes a Louis Vuitton handbag worth the sticker price to its purchaser is the unique set of expectations that that customer forms with

the brand. It is the emotional impact the Louis Vuitton products bring to the customer that other companies can't. If you buy a handbag from Louis Vuitton, you aren't just buying a solution to the problem of transporting your things from one place to another; you are buying the unique expectations and relationship that only Louis Vuitton offers—the historic prestige of Audrey Hepburn with the style of the modern "fashionista." What a Louis Vuitton bag says about the owner of that bag *plus* the relationship the customer has with the name Louis Vuitton is what creates the strong emotional-value for that audience.

To demonstrate this point further, imagine if Louis Vuitton decided to enter the furniture business. What would you expect of a Louis Vuitton couch? Quality? Pretentiousness? Prestige? Luxury? Style? Ritz? Glamour? Why or why wouldn't you buy one? Your answer to those questions explains your personal relationship with Louis Vuitton and the expectations, attributes, and qualities that you associate with that name— the essence of emotional-value.

This isn't just true of the luxury industry alone. Emotional-value plays a role in your brand perceptions every day. It's the difference between American Airlines and Virgin Airlines; Jif Peanut Butter and Skippy; American Express and Discover; Nike and Adidas; American Apparel and Gap. No matter what industry you are in, your customers will form a set of expectations about their relationship with you. It is up to you to help shape that relationship in a way that sets you apart from the rest of the market and creates a unique emotional-value. All the activities you do—resulting in your brand—are responsible for creating emotional-value for your audience.

So, what makes you unique? What does your company help your audience become that no other company can? What do your customers expect out of your products, customer service or marketing? These form the basis for an understanding of emotional-value and must be built upon the "who you are?" and "why you matter?" questions we covered earlier.

EXPANDING YOUR VALUE LENS

Both functional-value and emotional-value are necessary for break-through success. Together they form the basis for what your customers will be willing to pay for your offering. Both have a significant impact on the way you will go about developing your business and your brand. Sometimes the emotional-value will be the driving force behind what you are building, and other times it's the functional-value; but both are vital to delivering your value to your audience.

Cesar Hidalgo, a professor at MIT, uses the example of a Lockheed Martin F-22 Raptor to illustrate the concept of value. The F-22 is considered the most outstanding fighter plane ever built[40]. It's a single-seat, twin-engine fifth-generation super-maneuverable fighter aircraft using stealth technology.

The F-22 Raptor is an extremely expensive machine with a sticker price well over $150 million. To buy an F-22, you need a lot of money. An F-22 is also very complex. Lots of parts, pieces, and technologies come together to make it fly. Because of its complexity, the F-22 requires a lot of people with a lot of different types of expertise to produce.

If you take the price of an F-22 ($150,000,000) and divide it by its weight (43,340 lbs), the cost comes out to $3,461.01 a pound. That's somewhere between the price of silver and gold!

Now, take an F-22 and crash it into a mountain, or in the ocean, or blow it up into tiny little bits and fragments. How valuable is it now? It's probably way less valuable than silver, certainly less valuable than gold. In fact, in pieces, the scrap material is almost worthless. To the customer, it's absolutely worthless. Where is the value?

As Professors Michael E. Porter and Mark Kramer pointed out in the *Harvard Business Review*, "companies themselves remain trapped in an outdated approach to value creation that has emerged over the past few decades. They continue to view value creation narrowly, optimizing short-term financial performance in a bubble while missing the most important customer needs and ignoring the broader influences that determine their longer-term success."[41]

To give yourself the best chance at long-term success, you have to create emotional-value with your brand development. In any endeavor seeking to create value, there is no possible way to determine how your customers will perceive your worth independent of their emotional connection to you. Which means you must plan for, work at, and constantly experiment with ways to discover the emotional preferences and connections you are creating in the marketplace.

But how do you discover what your brand is worth? How do you evaluate its value? After all, how do you determine the value of your relationship with your mother? Or your spouse? Or your best friend? Even more, how will you measure the emotional-value you create for your customers? How will you test? Most importantly, how can you create a sustainable business model that consistently delivers emotional-value to your customers?

To answer these questions, you must dive deep. You have to go below the surface to see into the relational connections being created. This means innovation accounting on an emotional-value level. To be effective, you must get in front of your audience and discover the value being created through your *Value Stream.*

VALUE STREAM DISCOVERY

As we've discussed, brand development doesn't occur independently from the rest of the business. In *The Lean Entrepreneur*, Cooper-Vlaskovits introduced the *Value Stream Discovery* framework to expose assumptions about how an organization creates and delivers value. As Cooper put it, "The bottom line is that if people have no path to your product or service, then you will not be able to provide value to these people. They won't become your customer."

They argue a startup can look at its development through a series of steps to discover the value that is being created for the customer. By positing one best-case scenario, and working to validate that scenario, a startup can best understand the pathway to capturing a market.

The game Angry Birds is a great way to understand the Value Stream. Do you remember when you first heard about Angry Birds? Did you discover on it your own? Was it introduced to you via a friend or family member? Perhaps you were introduced to it in the app store as one of the "Top Free Apps" or "Featured Apps." Then you downloaded the free version (MVP) because you were curious and you thought it looked like fun. You wanted to know what the fuss was about. Then you enjoyed playing the game so much, you couldn't wait to get Angry Birds Space or Angry Birds Star Wars, and you bought the paid version.

Then you put it on your homescreen because you played it so much. Then you decided you'd buy all future Angry Bird games, because you trust they'll be awesome. Then, you bought the T-shirt or the stuffed animal, because Angry Birds is "your thing" and told all of your friends and co-workers that they were missing out by not downloading the newest Angry Birds Epic.

Although Angry Birds is a microcosm of the Value Stream, it is a great way to understand the way your customers will move from becoming aware of you to becoming passionate about you.

In Cooper's model, there are five parts of any innovation endeavor that must be validated to prove that it's ready to scale. Each of these parts

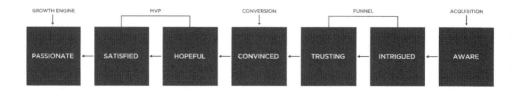

can be represented by one or more 'states' the customer goes through. Founders hypothesize what 'activity' the business must conduct in order to help the customer transition to the next state, what behavior the customer performs to indicate the transition, and how to measure the behavior.

When you add an emotional-value component to the Value Stream Discovery framework, you begin to see just how integrated brand (emotional-value) and product (functional-value) are in each stage of a startup's development.

Acquisition

In the acquisition channel, you first reach out to your customers and they become *aware* of you. In an early stage startup, this is likely done through a low-cost marketing activity, such as Google AdWords, SEO, or blogging. This first touch is the first introduction to your brand. In more established startups, customers may "hear about you." This is an example of brand actually being responsible for awareness.

At "Awareness", customers ask themselves questions like, "Are they talking to me?" "Do I fit in?" "Am I attracted to this?" These questions are less about your product (which hasn't been experienced yet) and more about an invitation to participate in your brand. At this point, you are making your first relational introductions with your customers and they are deciding whether or not you are worth considering a relationship with.

Someone has winked at you from across the room.

Funnel

In the funnel, activities taken by the business develop a rapport with the audience. The rapport is represented by two states, "Intrigued" and "Trusting." Intrigued is that a potential customer comes to believe that the product, if all it's said to be, would satisfy a need. Trusting is that the customer believes the business is sincere and capable of delivering on the functional promise of the product.

How you interact with your customers and how they respond to you are an integral part of your intentional branding. In the funnel, the forming relationship starts to become a driving force behind a customer trusting you or not trusting you in the journey toward crossing the threshold of actually paying for your product or service (the penny gap).

Intrigue and trusting are often emotional responses to the story you're telling and your brand artifacts. The customer needn't consciously say, "Gee, this product sure seems like it will solve my deep emotional need to feel special!" But the messaging you use must promise product utility, plus invite the customer on a shared journey to achieve an emotional impact:

> Your children will love music like you do
> Your boss will view you as a hero
> You will feel like a better husband
> Your mommy's group will recognize you as a great mother
> You will be seen as an industry thought-leader

The person who winked at you strikes up a conversation; is flirting with you.

Conversion

When a customer crosses the penny gap, it is rarely a purely rational proposition. When a customer decides to pull out a credit card and pay, the relationship with you plays a strong role in their decision. Customers, both in consumer and business products, are flooded with information about alternatives, features, and benefits. Your values, what you aspire your customer to be—the story you tell—ultimately play a huge role in *convincing* customers to choose you over other products and provides a pathway for developing a relationship beyond your initial transaction.

You decide to go out on a date.

MVP

The MVP is your proposed *minimum viable product* to fulfill the value proposition of your product. In this part of the model, the product is the driving force behind your customer being "Hopeful" that they've made the right choice to address their needs and ultimately "Satisfied" that the functional promise made at the "Intrigue" state has been fulfilled.

You try to provide value to customers; you try to address a specific need. The dilemma is that before you have someone using your product, you don't know what the exact need is or how to exactly address it. The MVP starts with your first proposal at sufficiently addressing the need. The more you build the less you understand what is required! Iteratively building and validating increases your understanding of customer need and product functionality required.

MVP versions are released to small cohorts of customers (your early adopters), which are grown iteratively as knowledge increases.

Make no mistake: bad product experiences adversely affect your relationship with your audience. That's why MVP releases are not "launched" to the wide market. In this context, your early adopters are those who are willing to persist in a relationship with you despite an imperfect product experience in the shared quest for value. The more mature the MVP, the more integrated branding artifacts are into the experiments.

As you're headed to the restaurant, you hope you've made the right choice. By the end of the night, the Minimum Viable Date is one in which maybe not everything was perfect, but there's a good indication that the two of you might be a match. Over time, if successful, the MVD evolves into a long-term relationship. It's no longer minimal. It's beyond viable.

Growth Engine

Nowhere does brand play a bigger role in the Value Stream Discovery model than in the growth engine. The relationship you have formed with your customer from Awareness to Satisfaction is your brand. The relationship determines whether your customer is "Passionate" about you and your offering or not. If they are passionate, they will share their experience with others. They will give you positive reviews, act as references, provide testimonials, show you off, or pay high margins. In effect, passionate customers become willing or unwilling ambassadors for your startup.

They become your *engine of growth*. (More on this in Chapter 10).

Growth comes from the shared aspiration inherent in the relationship the audience forms with you. Your brand is the mechanism for inciting passion and the shared journey of fulfilling that aspiration with your audience.

PATHWAY TO ENGAGEMENT

The relationship between audience and organization is typically formed in order from awareness to passionate. But this is not how a startup endeavor validates the value it's attempting to create. If the product doesn't work, or doesn't fulfill the promise you've been making, you're putting the chances of a valuable relationship at risk. People are going to feel a certain way about your product. They may be angry, they may be happy, they may be complacent, or inspired, or just plain mean. Human emotion explains why people who have a bad experience with a product are much more likely to spread the word than people who have had a good experience with the same product[42].

If the product experience is positive, then the resulting impact on the relationship will be positive. If the product experience is below satisfaction, then the resulting impact on the relationship will also be less than satisfied. Customers who have moved from awareness to trusting are valuable. You do not have an unlimited supply of customers, and a customer lost has to become a lesson learned. The point here is your product has to deliver.

Therefore, the startup must validate the MVP first. To do this, you must start forming relationships with your intended audience. This is the perfect time to test your intentional branding using your Minimum Viable Brand (MVB): story, artifacts, and invitation—while also discovering what is required to deliver the promised value.

Again, brand development can't be thought of as independent from the overall goals of the business. Instead, you have to think about brand, product, marketing, sales, customer service, and so on, as one integrated customer experience. Remember the F-22? All the customer sees is the jet, not the stream you've created to put the jet in front of them.

For each step, you wish the customer to move on to the next step. You want them to take a specific action. From the customer's perspective, the stream should create an overall flow or pathway for engagement with the organization. From the organization's perspective, you must do something or have something to lead the customer down the stream of actions.

The goal, then, is to posit one best-case scenario in which a customer moves from the beginning of the stream all the way through the stream in a fluid series of customer-action—resulting business action, customer-action—resulting business action, and so on down the stream. If you can't move people from one step to the next, it's not going to help you to start over from the beginning with new customers without changing anything. In other words, you must *optimize the value stream from the inside out.*

VALIDATE YOUR LEARNINGS

To optimize your value stream, you must build upon validated learning. How will you learn what is valuable in your efforts and what is wasteful? How will you discover where to push and where to retreat? How will you learn if and when people form a relationship with your brand?

Learning is the essential unit of progress for any brand development. Validated learning is the system that allows the decision makers of the organization to prove objectively the iterations they are making to their brand development are having a measurable impact on the value being delivered to their customers.

As the conventional branding model has proven time and again, it's easy to kid yourself about what you think your audience wants. Take for example the "Got Milk?" campaign. The American Dairy Association's huge success with its "Got Milk?" campaign prompted them to expand advertising to Mexico. However, the Spanish translation they entered the Mexican market with read, "Are you lactating?" Or consider Nestlé's first official Instagram photo featuring their new mascot bear playing a drum set. As it turned out, their new mascot bore an uncanny resemblance to Pedobear, the unofficial pedophilia mascot.

It's also easy to learn things that are completely irrelevant or unhelpful in forming your relationships. As such, validated learning is backed up by empirical evidence collected from real, living people. Adding an emotional-value lens to the Value Stream Discovery model gives you a dynamic way to learn about the value being created in the context of the overall business, but only if you can measure the activities undertaken in the stream.

Measuring human emotion and human relationship is a difficult task. There are no direct or completely reliable metrics to provide you with completely accurate measurements of people's emotions, feelings, and ultimately their relationship with you. There are, however, ways to get a clear picture of how people are relating to your organization.

When measuring the emotional-value your brand development efforts are creating, you must look for and discover the *live wires*. Live wires are the places where people light up with who you are and what you stand for; where people are compelled to join with you and your story, and where people are willing to evangelize for your cause. Proof of a live wire is best viewed through the lens of three emotional-value metrics: *interaction*, *engagement*, and *participation*.

EMOTIONAL-VALUE METRICS: INTERACTION, ENGAGEMENT, PARTICIPATION

Emotional-value is much deeper than what shows on the surface. Remember, people create allegiances and loyalty to brands through underlying sets of expectations and preferences about the relationships they choose to form with any organization. These emotional preferences are the proof points to discovering the value in your intentional brand development efforts.

Not all emotional-value is the same. There are varying depths to your relationships with your customers and each has its own emotional-value attached to it. Although there are a myriad of ways to look at it, the most useful way of understanding your depth of emotional-value is to view it through the metrics around interaction, engagement, and participation. These will clarify and strengthen your recognition of how people relate to you and what that means for your brand's development.

As emotional preferences and expectations get clearer, so does the relationship. As the relationship gets clearer, so does your emotional-value. And, as we've seen, when you overlay emotional-value metrics on top of the value stream, you can get a clearer picture of how branding plays a role in the overall development of the business.

As you experiment in the development of your brand, these metrics are a useful way to single out transitional spaces where your relationships begin to move deeper and farther towards passion. You can identify places where your relationships are stagnating and iterate to create fluent transitions to help people deepen their emotional bond with you. You must work to move people from being passive observers of your organization to being active participants in your story. This means optimizing your brand elements (via an MVB) to move people from interaction to engagement and finally to participation.

Interaction

Interaction is the starting point of any relationship. It simply says, "I like that" or "I connect with that." Interaction is typically the result of good messaging and medium choices. The message connects with a customer and they feel affiliation for what it has to say.

The measure of interaction is whether or not a customer takes an action based on your emotional-value offering. Does someone click the link? Do they walk through the doors? Do they watch the video? Do they open the email? Based on what you have offered, can you get a customer to activate?

Interaction is only a surface indication of emotional-value. Customers may "like" tons of companies they have never purchased products from. In truth, people interact with a multitude of brands. Interaction is a

non-exclusive, open-minded relationship that allows a customer to "flirt" with an organization and what they stand for without committing to a real relationship. (You may have taken an Audi for a test-drive, but you might not own one.)

Often, too many organizations simply stop at interaction. "People really like me!" Don't mistake interaction for the depth of emotional-value you can and should attain. Interaction is a starting point, not the end point of a relationship with your customers. To discover value, you must go deeper than simple clicks and likes and dig into the reasons behind these actions.

Interaction can be a game of big numbers, and big numbers can make you feel good. After all, who doesn't like the feeling of having 200k "fans?" But big numbers can also be extremely misleading. Interaction metrics like follower count, fan count, page visits, likes, and upvotes are what Eric Ries calls *vanity metrics* (easily manipulated metrics that do not necessarily correlate to the numbers that really matter: active users, engagement, the cost of getting new customers, and ultimately revenues and profits). The relative value of 10,000 Twitter followers with 100 engaged people is the same as a Twitter following of 100 with 100 engaged people.

Engagement

Engagement is the next depth of emotional-value. It says, "I want that," or "I desire that." Engagement is typically the result of great differentiation or a disruptive product offering. People have a choice in who they choose to engage when comparing one brand against another. Which means, who a customer chooses to engage with is an affirmation of your positioning against competitors or the sprouting of a new market altogether. Good branding incites engagement.

For new ventures, volume doesn't inherently create engagement. For a startup, without an established brand and an unknown market and customers, the objective of your brand development is to discover and build a relevant audience. That means a startup that can create real engagement through validated learning can leverage that engagement into equal footing (market equity) with much larger companies.

The measure of engagement is a person's response to an interaction with you. Engagement is about the quality of the interaction and how far someone is willing to go once they've interacted with your brand. Will a customer give you their email address? Do they sign up to pre-order? Do they sponsor your crowdfunding campaign? Does someone comment on your post?

If interaction is speed dating, engagement is (as the old-timers say) "going steady." When a customer chooses to engage with you, they are giving something back in response to your offer.

Although engagement proves a clear level of value, it can be deceivingly temporary. To truly measure engagement, you must look to the emotional, cognitive, and behavioral connections that exist over time. If your relationship stagnates at the engagement level, all it takes is another company to come along with a more enticing offer at the right time to lure your customers away from you. Engagement alone cannot sustain your emotional-value in the long run.

Participation

Participation is the deepest depth of relationship. It says, "I am part of that," or "I am the same as that." Participation is the powerful blend of your story, your artifacts, inviting people to join you, authenticity, and trust over time. When a person decides to participate they are identifying with who you are, what you stand for, and where you are going. They're not just happy you've filled a need; they're thankful it was you who did it and are excited to join you in where you are headed.

The functional-value and emotional-value of your offering are amplified by a customer's willingness to participate in the experience. Participation represents an invitation to co-creation, co-responsibility, and co-delight. Participation gears toward one objective—passion.

The measure of participation may be the least concrete of all three metrics, yet people who are truly, devotedly passionate about you do exhibit certain measurable behaviors. A passionate person is more likely to brag to their friends and family about you. A passionate person is more likely to feel pride in their purchase. A passionate person is more likely to actively recruit others to the cause.

While it's true you cannot put an absolute numerical value on the feeling of passion, you can certainly create proxy questions—validated over time—around the behaviors associated with passion. Does a customer brag about their purchase? Does someone consistently show up to your events? Does a customer actively evangelize for your startup? What is your net promoter score? What is your must-have score? Are case studies being written about you? Are press releases being received? What do your customers' testimonials tell you?

Participation boils down to the level of passion a particular group of people has with you. To create passionate advocates for your organization, you must create a great experience, entice people to join with you, and then engage with them on a regular basis to deepen and solidify your relationships.

When someone participates they can begin to take on the identity of your brand, reaching that fascinating place where terms like "Mac-Guy," "Coke-lover," and "Gucci-Girl" enter the story. It's also the place where Harley-Davidson tattoos and naming your children "Twitter" or "Facebook" might make sense (to some). The line between you and your audience becomes blurred. Every startup should focus on optimizing its brand development for participation. It is the most potent relationship you can have.

People define themselves everyday with the brands they choose to buy, wear, use, and promote. It's where brands almost become a sort of religious experience and people turn into brand evangelists and spokespeople. It's all in, full-blown, no holds barred emotional-value. If interaction is speed dating and engagement is "going steady," identity is a committed life-long marriage.

Apple recently unseated Coca-Cola's 13 year run as the world's most valuable brand in Interbrand's coveted annual "World's Most Valuable Brands" list[43]. This can't solely be attributed to disruptive tech releases. In fact, from 2007–2008 (the release of the iPhone), Apple's brand value ranking only jumped 9 slots (from 33rd to 24th). So what took Apple's brand value from $13,583m to $98,316m in 5 years? Passionate participation.

Think about it, their entire model is centered around the invitation of participation. Participation from independent third parties (apps, hacks, media); participation from partner industries (music publishing, cellular carriers, media producers); and, most of all, participation from their customers. Apple exemplifies participation by placing it at the nexus of everything it does. This level of participation has created passionate evangelists skyrocketing Apple's value over the last 5 years.

HOW TO MEASURE EMOTIONAL-VALUE

All of this happens within the context of the larger business objectives. If people interact with a brand's value offering, they start to become aware of what the brand is, possibly become intrigued by the story or the rallying point of the brand, and become trusting of what the brand stands for. As they move from interaction to engagement, they become convinced the brand is for them, hopeful that by joining the brand they will feel validated, and become satisfied if the brand delivers on the promise it has made to them. As people become passionate about a brand, they begin to participate with the brand, "seeing" themselves as a part of the aspirations for the brand. They begin to share their passion with their friends, neighbors, coworkers, and the like to create a growth engine for the organization.

All measurement is observing and tracking real customers' behavior. Of course, the most direct and powerful way to measure is to get outside of your building and in front of your customers. Getting outside of the building is a way to figure out why your audience behaves in a certain way. If you are not out meeting with the people who may someday become your customers, and learning about their needs, their challenges and their dreams, you are probably buying into the classic "Field of Dreams fallacy"—thinking, "if we build it they will come." If you fail to truly understand what makes your customers tick, you will most certainly do one of three things: build too much, build the wrong thing, or deliver too late.

Recall, when undertaking new endeavors statistical significance isn't the goal. You're looking for one group of passionate customers—one cohort—to be able to turn that into a sustainable market.

Most businesses can figure out ways to measure much of their value stream through online activity. On the Internet, you are only limited by your creativity. Your customers will do something that will indicate they have moved from one step to another in the value stream. In some cases this can be done with a simple analytics tool, and in others you will have to be much more clever.

When it comes to measuring emotional-value, the human brain truly is the best analytical tool. Don't just rely on the tools and expect them to give you a full picture. For example, the only real way to measure engagement and how people are feeling about your story, channel, messaging, and relevance is to analyze the conversations yourself.

What are people saying to you on your channels? Is it positive? Is it hostile? Is it neutral? Who is saying it? Your audience? Trolls? Bloggers? Early adopters? Track these conversations over time, and this will allow you to track your emotional-value growth over time. You will also be able to learn about what is not working and what is working to address it head on.

This means being able to connect the dots from multiple data points generated throughout your organization. It means being able to see beyond the vanity metrics and into the relational metrics that are creating value for your customers.

Experiment often, fail quickly, measure your learnings, validate your assumptions, and build on what works.

PARTICIPATION ⟶

ENGAGEMENT ⟶

INTERACTION ⟶

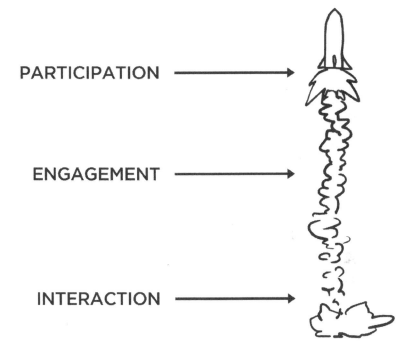

CHAPTER 9

WADING IN: VIABILITY EXPERIMENTS

GOODBYE, OLD-SCHOOL MARKET RESEARCH

Every brand starts with a certain set of assumptions ranging from the most likely type of person to become passionate about you to the emotional response your audience has to a certain set of actions you take in the value stream. If the conventional branding model thought of these assumptions at all, they were typically tested through varying surface level forms of "market research" conducted in focus groups, surveys, or other forms of traditional market research.

Yet, this type of research rarely, if ever, provides any of the insights needed for a startup to develop and grow their brand. As Harvard Business School Professor Jerry Zaltman writes, "To the extent that we structure the stimulus—whether it's a discussion guide in a focus group or a question in a survey—all people can do is respond. And there's value in that. But I see those as strip-mining techniques. Sometimes the valuable ore is on the surface. But often it's not. Strip-mining techniques are inappropriate when there's a great deal more depth to be had. Typically, the deeper you go, the more value there is."[44]

Traditional market research suffers from the "DVR effect." Think about what you have, right now, on your DVR at home. If you ask most people what television shows they DVR, they'll probably tell you something like, "Rachel Maddow, *Downtown Abbey*, and maybe *The Daily Show*, or *The Colbert Report*." and that's it. But when they get home and actually check their DVR recordings, they suddenly realize they also watch the Kardashians, *Sportscenter*, and have a backlog of *Duck Dynasty* episodes cued up. It's not that they were lying to you, it's that they didn't even realize they had these shows recorded.

Author Malcolm Gladwell explains the faultiness of this type of market research using a cup of coffee.[45] If you ask most people what type of coffee they drink, they'll probably say, "I like a bold, strong, full-bodied, and rich roast." But the truth is, when most people get their rich, bold coffee; what's the next thing they do? Head straight for the cream and sugar. The truth is, most people like milky, sweet, weak coffee. Again, people aren't lying; they are just limited to the extent and structure of the question.

Not only does traditional market research provide surface-level results and biased data, it is more often than not extremely costly and time consuming for an early endeavor to undertake. Take a focus group for example. Focus group costs typically include a moderator's fees, the cost of providing a facility, the cost of developing the questions, the cost of incentivizing respondents, and the costs of recruiting them in the first place. But a startup has neither the skill nor expertise to conduct a successful focus group on its own. As a result, they hire a professional firm to conduct the research for them, only driving up costs significantly. One such firm estimates the cost to range from $4000 to $8300. That's a lot to spend in a two-hour timeframe to produce shaky results at best.

Not only expensive, but traditional market research tends to extract the surface artifacts of the brand from the overall offering of the whole relationship. Facilitators may suggest testing the color scheme independent from the logo, or the logo independent from the product, or different artifacts in pieces. This type of testing only creates data in relation to a specific, narrow question, not to the most pertinent question a startup needs to answer—where's the value? Traditional market research is either too narrow or too broad to get the right picture of the value being created.

Goodbye, old-school market research. Hello, viability experiments.

HELLO, VIABILITY EXPERIMENTS

Today, Dyson makes the best- selling vacuum cleaner in the United States but Sir James Dyson ran over 5,126 experiments to finally get it right[46]. Tim Westergren approached over 300 investors, tweaking his idea and pitch each time, before he found funding for Pandora. Even Sly himself (Sylvester Stallone) was rejected over 1500 times before he got backing for the iconic film 'Rocky.'[47] If history teaches us anything, it's that winners experiment.

The startup world is full of seemingly instant successes. From the outside, it seems that founders simply hack together a website, write a few lines of code, and the next day thousands of users roll in. That may be true for the lucky 1%; but for the other 99%, we must learn how to experiment.

Just like a scientist runs experiments to prove or disprove a theory, or an engineer uses experiments to improve his design, or an athlete experiments to find the best training regiment; to test the business assumptions of your startup, you must be willing to experiment, learn, and experiment again. In the Lean Brand framework, these tests are called *viability experiments*.

The basic idea behind a viability experiment is to validate your assumptions by augmenting what customers say they're going to do with tests to show what they actually will do. The faster you can determine a failed approach or a winning approach, the quicker you can iterate or amplify that approach.

No matter where you are in your business journey, whether you're just getting started or have been in business for years, experimentation can help to iterate your offering and discover value for your audience. It is never too late to change an artifact, update your story, reword an invitation, or tighten your focus. Even if you're a startup with a strong relationship with your audience, even if you've breezed through the book so far feeling confident you're doing all you can, you can be doing more experiments.

The goal of any viability experiment is to generate learning, not to simply execute on what you believe to be true. As such, experiments should be expressed in a hypothesis-driven formula:

We believe if we [X] to [these people] we will achieve [this outcome]. We will know we are successful when we see [this signal from the market].

For example, perhaps you want to test your rally point (what you're fighting against and what you're fighting for). You could phrase the experiment like this:

We believe if we pitch our rally point via a meetup group, 10 people will want our contact information. We will know we are successful when 10 people are willing to ask for our contact information.

Or perhaps you want to test the viability of a brand artifact such as a photograph. You could phrase it like this,

We believe if we share this photo, 25 people within 2 hours will share it in their social feed. We will know we are successful when 25 people share.

Or perhaps you want to test the viability of an artifact such as packaging. You could phrase it like this,

> *We believe if we use this packaging as opposed to that packaging, 15 more customers an hour will stop to investigate our product offering. We will know we are successful when 15 more people investigate our product / hour.*

Recall, customers don't divide their perceptions about value in the same way a business can divide their attempts at value creation. Instead, a customer only views the value of an offering through the lens of the whole offering. As such, it's important to think about your viability experiments as holistic rather than independent tests. The best experiments yielding the best learnings, take into account the entire offering of both product and brand, not just part.

What follows are the most familiar and integrated methods of running viability experiments to validate your assumptions with your audience. No matter which experiments you choose to run, viability experimentation should become a part of the core DNA of your organization. Continuous experimentation leads to continuous learning which will improve your ability to deliver the most value to your audience in the best ways possible.

THE INFAMOUS LANDING PAGE, BRAND EDITION

In the startup world, the landing page test is perhaps the most widely used experiment. It is both easy and relatively inexpensive. The basic premise of a landing page experiment is to deploy a one-page website articulating your product offering, drive traffic to the page, call the user to some sort of action (typically an opt-in list), and then measure the conversion rate relative to the traffic rate.

Sounds simple enough, but there are multiple variables at play in any landing page experiment. How good is the customer acquisition method? What intrigued someone to visit in the first place? How well is the value proposition articulated for the acquired audience? How well do the design elements tell the startup's story?

While a landing page is an easy and quick way to begin testing your assumptions, you should have clear goals and a clear understanding of what you're trying to learn before you put it up.

Acquisition

Consider the "TechCrunch Bump" (the surge in traffic and awareness typically experienced after a startup gets coverage in TechCrunch). The bump is well documented and is coveted by many startups, but what does the bump teach you about your brand?[48] What types of people are subscribing? What aspect of your story enticed them to click on the link? More importantly, why did they subscribe? Did the article tell the right story? Did people engage with the story we are telling?

Certainly alternative media and channels exist which you might wish to explore when it comes to discovering the best way to make people aware that you exist. If the types of people you believe will be most passionate about you are on TechCrunch, then get on TechCrunch! But if not, chances are there are better channels more indicative of the personas you are trying to reach.

Remember, when it comes to testing your brand, the medium through which a person becomes aware of you can say as much as the page they end up visiting. Finding the right acquisition channel is as important as acquiring subscribers. Learning about a product through Lifehacker. com is different than learning about a product through Oprah. A startup should focus on deciphering the medium through which they will acquire the right users. Absent a clear understanding of medium, the results of a landing page test can become quickly skewed.

Design Elements

Design may be an important aspect of your product offering. Great UX and intuitive UI are becoming more and more the rule rather than the exception. Yet, most landing pages are pretty bland and follow a pretty predictable formula. Product photo, catchy strapline, a list of benefits called "game changing" below the fold, and an opt-in form placed in the header.

There is a lot of research behind this formula, but just because the formula is considered "best practice" doesn't mean it is actually giving you data that you can learn from. In other words, you have to ask the question, "best practice for what result?" Is the result opt-ins? Is the result load time? Is the result looking nice?

To test the viability of your brand, the result has to include a measurement of emotional-value. If you look beyond simple vanity metrics, there

are lots of ways to integrate interaction, engagement, and participation metrics into a landing page experiment.

To do so, start asking yourself these questions:

Does our landing page tell a complete story?

Does it use imagery other than our product to engage the audience?

Does it contain enough depth to be able to measure participation?

What are we asking the user to engage with?

How is our unique rallying point represented in the founder's story or in the product description?

How can we obtain qualitative feedback?

If you leave variables like layout, acquisition, and product description the same, you can easily run A/B tests (testing two versions of an element, A and B, with a metric that defines success) directed at learning about the effectiveness and engagement of these different emotional-value elements.

Post Subscribe

When you've driven the right people to the page, have nailed the design elements, successfully articulated your value hypothesis to your visitors, and successfully intrigued people to subscribe, what's next? Very simply, you have to start the work of understanding what people engaged with and why. Typically, this information is only discoverable if you're willing to ask. The best and most direct way to learn is to send a personal email and ask to have a conversation. Using customer development or other customer empathy devices, you should be able to learn what someone engaged with and why they did.

Additionally, you could employ a simple drip campaign, or use a "high-hurdle" test (making it relatively tough—or high-hurdle—for potential customers to engage) to enhance what you can learn from a landing page test.

Most importantly, you want to understand the reasons behind the behavior, not just settle for the behavior itself. Understanding the reasons—rational or irrational—behind why a customer chose to take an action on your landing page can lead to valuable insights into how to go about developing long-term relationships with your customers and build traction with your early adopters.

CROWDFUNDING EXPERIMENT

Crowdfunding sites like Kickstarter, GoFundMe, Indiegogo, RocketHub, and Publishizer (the crowdpublishing platform we used to launch this book) are experiencing rapid growth worldwide. Crowdfunding platforms raised $2.7 billion (an 81% increase over 2011) and successfully funded more than 1 million campaigns in 2012. In 2013, global crowdfunding volumes rose to $5.1 billion[49]. By 2020, crowdfunding volumes are projected to contribute $500 billion in funding per year generating $3.2 trillion plus in economic value per year[50]. Orange isn't the new black, crowdfunding is!

If you're unfamiliar, the basic premise of crowdfunding is to collaboratively finance an idea, product, feature, or other work via a temporary online campaign (typically 1–2 months). There are essentially two main models of crowdfunding. The first—and most common—is donation-based funding, where funders donate towards a collaborative goal in return for the actual product, rewards, or differing perks. The second is investment-based funding, where businesses seeking capital sell ownership in their startup in the form of equity or debt. Although currently only available to accredited investors, the horizon for investment-based crowdfunding is growing.

Crowdfunding experiments provide an incredible platform to test the assumptions of an organization in a very integrated way, testing multiple variables in your value offering at the same time. Most importantly, a crowdfunding experiment asks a potential customer to cross the penny gap based on the value proposition expressed by the startup running the campaign without having yet built the product.

Kickstarter outlines their recommendations for a successful campaign in very clear intentional Lean Brand development tones:

"Tell us who you are. Tell us the story behind your project. Where'd you get the idea? What stage is it at now? How are you feeling about it? *[Story]*

Come out and ask for people's support, explaining why you need it and what you'll do with their money. *[Invitation]*

Talk about how awesome your rewards are, using any images you can. *[Artifacts]*

Explain that if you don't reach your goal, you'll get nothing, and everyone will be sad.

Thank everyone!

And don't be afraid to put your face in front of the camera and let people see who they're giving money to. We've watched thousands of these things, and you'd be surprised what a difference this makes."[51]

Not surprisingly, all of these recommendations directly relate to your Lean Brand development efforts. Tell people who you are, the story behind the project, and attempt to connect on an emotional, relational level—all brand elements you will be developing in versions of your MVB. There are all sorts of options when it comes to testing your brand through a crowdfunding campaign.

For example, you could test the emotional-value of your rally point by gearing your entire video around articulating and demonstrating what you're fighting for. Or you could test secondary artifacts through the add-on rewards. Or you could even test engagement by opening up a comments section on the campaign site. The options are only limited by your creativity.

As with all viability experiments, the goal is to validate the assumptions you've made about the value being delivered to your customers through your offering, not just to successfully fund a round of production. If your campaign was successful, don't stop there. Push deeper into why people were convinced enough to pull out their credit cards and preorder your product. What lead them to the page and made them aware of your existence in the first place? What intrigued them about your offering? Why did they choose to participate? Were they passionate enough to share the campaign with their friends and family?

If your campaign is unsuccessful, find out which elements of your offering failed to create value. Which elements didn't spark engagement? Which elements worked? Did people understand the offering or did they misinterpret what you were trying to say? Why? Then learn from the information, reload, and try it again.

VIABILITY EXPERIMENTS IN A SOCIAL GOOD COMMUNITY

An Interview With Parker Harris (Co-founder & President)

Junto Global is a social venture that organizes communities of peers and friends who seek to better themselves and the greater global community. Junto has been successful in building an incredible, engaged community that spans the globe. Parker Harris, Co-founder & President of Junto Global, shares some of the work behind building his organization, how his audience has grown through experimentation, and his advice on how to build a passionate community.

TLB: Junto is an interesting name. Where did it come from and what is Junto Global?

Junto, by definition, means to "join together." Junto, as a social venture, is a community of peers that come together to better themselves, better the world, and grow intellectually. It's a space for talented, passionate people to connect, grow, and contribute. Junto provides the tools, resources, and experiences to help its members assess where they are and where they want to go, set a plan to get there, and empower them along the way.

TLB: Your product is really a community of people. How has your community evolved into what it is today?

We started with this really special interdisciplinary core group from the beginning. It was the same psychographic of people, but very different in other ways, with this pure interest from the beginning that allowed a very special mix of ideas to unfold and allowed people to experience results in a variety of sectors of their life together.

What I've learned is that successful ideas don't come from the outside; they come from the inside. From this core group of 30–45 people, people began moving into different geographies. If they had the right set of skills and talents, they were able to start their own Junto group within their local area. That's how we grew. We've done very little to control the growth, but instead, we've focused on how to empower it and harness that intentionally.

TLB: That last sentence is a really powerful idea. Can you go a bit deeper into what you mean by empowering and harnessing your organic growth versus controlling it?

The way I've come to think about it is that there are different values for different people that are a part of our organization. Customers—or in my case members, employees, and investors—are looking for transformation which is highlighted by growth. What is so powerful about Junto is that it meets different needs for different people along that path. So when you reach that transformational level with them it means your customers become evangelists and the organization is able to grow. Growth is just a testament to our structure, our framework, and the value we have learned that presents.

I have a huge admiration for a lot of really great organizations that are built around a community of people (or their audience) rather than a single person. Building something around a single person, or a couple of founders, is a terrible idea. With Junto, I wanted it to be built around our people, values, and culture rather than just around me.

TLB: That must be because, from a founder's perspective, Junto is your "baby." How do you know when to step in and move things along and when to be hands off and let things happen?

That's a great question. One of my life philosophies is to "love without attachment." Which means to sort of be removed from the outcome of the situation while showing love in the middle of the situation. That's how I try to approach our growth as much as possible. I try to look at it from the other person's perspective, which has taught me not to take things personally at all. Yes, I want to create an organization that helps people become successful in all aspects of life. Yes, I want to create an organization that helps you become successful if something is missing for you. It's not up to anybody else, that's up to me. But our growth is inherently about others, not about me.

TLB: That's a tough lesson.

Yeah, I know. I think that's a really tough lesson, but I don't have another option. I think there is a certain level of growth for any founder where, at some point, you feel like you can't rely on anybody else. But other people obviously have to be involved. What I've come to learn is this: don't do business with people that just buy what you have. Do business with people who believe what you believe.

I'm biased, but I think Junto is a solution for everyone's problem. I really feel that way and that's why we built it. But it's not just all about my perspective. It's not just about how I can build Junto, but also about how we can build Junto as a community. Through our learning, we have come to believe that people are interested in finding their passion and living their story without having to sacrifice family or health or some of the things that they are often asked to sacrifice. We also believe that we can help to make the world better in the process. All too often, we give up our health to get wealthy and then we give up all our wealth to get back to being healthy again. I think we've seen that as a broken model and I don't think our generation is going to fall for that trap as much.

TLB: There is also another type of balance to your growth. There's a microscopic view, which is the individual member, and there is a bigger view, which is Junto as an organization. How are you bringing all of these microscopic stories together to tell a bigger organizational story?

On an individual level, we are focused down to the core, single person. We provide tools, ways to measure success and impact, and processes to help you. We provide this methodology for analyzing where you are at and then help set rules to help you get where you want to go. Whether it's goal setting, or ways to analyze your life, or getting resources from us; we really provide space for individuals to connect with themselves. On an individual level, we work to create that space.

From an organizational level, we try to focus on our values. We have a very strong focus on community and fostering that community. One of the things we do, for example, is to do community events that are member driven. We want out members to be the force behind these events. If a member has an inspirational idea, that idea should turn into proactiveness about doing that event. It's great because it means that people are doing what they want to do and are contributing to our community in a way that they want to contribute. Those events are pretty foundational and serve as great experiments to learn about how we can better nurture our community.

The main focus, in everything we do, is to continue to deliver value to our current members and to make sure new members are getting the same value. I think it has always been important for us to protect that. It has always been a place where we could be very comfortable opening it up, and we want to make sure that as we grow, new people feel the same way. The people that are a part of Junto are admirable and authentic and real. When they are having a level of success in their lives based on what we are providing for them, then Junto is constantly in reference.

TLB: You've been successful in building a global community. Looking back, what advice would you give a new startup who is trying to build community?

Community is so important. Recently, a company in San Diego was purchased for three or four hundred million dollars by Otterbox. Basically they were a cell phone case company, and that was it. But, they built a community of people around the idea of being able to take technology everywhere and to have mobile technology in any situation. They literally grew to that extent in a three year period by building a community. I would say that building a community is the most painful thing you will ever have to do because it's like a product that can talk back to you . . . all the time.

To do it successfully, first, I would tell them to build it for themselves. Second, I'd tell them to do business with people who believe what you believe and to help people along their path that need your help. Third, I would say show up to places that you want to go not for what you're going to get out of it. All of this comes with learning about what works and what doesn't. That's how we were able to build a community of the "right" people at Junto. The "right" people are the people that are like you and like what you are doing and want to be a part of it.

THE IMPOSTER JUDO EXPERIMENT

The Imposter Judo experiment involves running an experiment using your competitors' products and is a great way to understand your customers' needs. Marty Neumeier in his influential book, *The Brand Gap*, takes this idea to brand development. Neumeier defines the test this way: "Swap part of your icon—the name or the visual element—with that of a competing brand, or even a brand from another category. If the resulting icon is better, or no worse than it was, your existing icon has room for improvement. By the same token, no other company should be able to improve its icon by using part of yours."[52]

Although an Imposter Judo test may be initially most valuable inside the organization, it can lead to insights about your brand outside of your walls just as easily. If you extend the test beyond your logo or icon, you can produce some very interesting results. Take your story for example. If you were to replace your organization's name with the name of a competitor in the heading of a few paragraphs about your story, would it still have as much meaning or less? Would your customers reject the story as untrue, or would they accept the story no matter the name in the copy? What does that say about you? Why?

Or take your visual artifacts. If you swap the imagery of a competitor with your imagery, does your brand still stand up? Do customers relate the same way? You can almost guarantee a failure in this test if you're using stock photography from sites like GettyImages.com or Stockphoto.com. That's because the imagery you are using isn't yours. What does an image from your organization look like? What makes it distinct? Why do people engage or not engage with your images? Why?

You can apply this type of test to your story elements, your tone of voice, all of your brand artifacts, and even to the mediums you choose to

communicate through. (If Tesla sold cars at Walmart, would they really be Tesla?)

The Imposter Judo test can provide a range of experiments with a wide variety of usage scenarios for you to learn from. Again, you are only limited by your imagination and creativity when it comes to testing. As with all experiments, it's important to define the hypothesis you are testing for each Judo test you run, learn from them, and iterate on your offering.

THE SMOKE TEST

An easy way to gauge intrigue and potential passion for your intentional branding efforts is to run a smoke test. Smoke tests are very basic experiments to try the validity of your potential emotional-value offering. They actually originated in the hardware testing practice of turning on a new piece of hardware for the first time and considering it a success if it does not catch fire and smoke. These tests are the simplest and most blunt tests in your experimentation arsenal.

To run an emotional-value smoke test, simply propose the value hypothesis and measure the results.

For example, you could post an ad on a site like Craigslist for your new music app saying, "Who's tired of Spotify commercials? We are too!" and add a simple call to action like, "email us for more info." If no one emails you, you're either testing with the wrong group of people or simply no one connected with your offering. If your inbox is overflowing, you're probably on to something.

Or invite people to a meetup around what you're fighting against and what you're fighting for. Do people show up? Do they invite their friends? Why? Or simply reach out to someone (not your mother, best friend, or brother) whom you believe would be passionate about your startup and buy them a cup of coffee. Smoke tests are only limited to how willing you are to interact with potential customers.

Although smoke tests are relatively simple, they act as an initial entry-way to learn about why people will potentially interact, engage, and eventually participate with your value offering. Successful smoke tests outline the specific hypothesis you are attempting to validate and the relational metrics you will use to measure its success or failure.

EXPERIMENT, EXPERIMENT, EXPERIMENT

Truly, there is no right way to learn. There's only not learning.

Experiments of all types can create insight for any startup endeavor as long as they produce measurable and insightful validated learning. The goal for any experiment is to test the assumptions being made in as realistic and expedient a way as possible. There is no bad way to learn, there is only learning and not learning.

Unlike cold statistics, emotional testing relies on discovering intuitively and empirically why someone took an action. The best way to figure out why is to simply ask. Remember, the human brain is the best analytical tool you have. By wading into emotional-value testing, you will be able to learn about what in your brand development is not working and what is working to address it head on.

To determine what you should test, draw from your business and brand assumptions, what is known vs. unknown, what you hypothesize will be big impact vs. small impact; and start with the one you need to learn the most about or is the weakest in the set. Identify the ways in which you can test, and then perform the test. If the results are robust enough to validate or invalidate your assumption, move on to the next. If not, find another way to test the assumption until you can prove the viability either way.

Every iteration on your MVB merits another round of audience feedback, so keep building a list of people willing to talk to you and finding places where you can go invite others into the conversation.

All startups should experiment. This is the only way to validate your assumptions in pursuit of building a sustainable, passionate relationship with your audience.

**DISRUPTING GOVERNMENT THROUGH TRIAL
& ERROR**

An Interview With Catherine Bracy (Director of Community
Organizing), Lauren Reid (Senior Public Affairs Manager),
and Kevin Curry (Director of the Brigade)

*Code For America (CFA) is shaking up the non-profit, gov-
ernment, and social good space. From their accelerator program
to their global peer network, Code For America has been helping
local governments solve social issues through technology. One of
their most successful programs, the Brigade, is a particularly interesting study in the right way to learn from your audience. They
shared some of their insights into how the Brigade got its start,
how they experimented to find value, and how they are managing
its growth.*

*TLB: For those that may not be familiar with you, give us the
basics. What is Code For America?*

Code For America is a service for the twenty-first century. We're working towards a government by the people, for
the people, of the people, and that works in the twenty-first

century using technology. We work to empower the people both inside and outside the government to harness technology to solve community problems. We do this through five core programs—the Fellowship, the Brigade, the Peer Network, the Accelerator Program, and then Code For All. It's really the people who make up these communities, more than anything else, that make us who we are.

TLB: What's fascinating is that all of these programs are volunteer driven and you're getting loads of volunteers to join you and take ownership in CFA. Specifically in the Brigade. Can you tell us about the Brigade and how it got it start?

It really starts with our Fellowship program. Through the Fellowship, we recruit web developers, urbanists, designers, and passionate citizens that have experience with technology to come and do a year of service with us. We partner them with municipal governments to spend a year in that community finding some technology solution to a problem that the government is having or that the community is having.

That program launched with a lot of attention and traction. Tim O'Reilly and a lot of others had started talking about Gov 2.0 and bringing that concept into the government space a few years before we launched. There were a lot of people there that were dissatisfied with where they were and were excited for the opportunity that the Fellowship presented them with. It was very popular, but had a very low acceptance rate. So there were hundreds of people who were super talented and smart who started collecting into a group of people who wanted to participate, but weren't in the Fellowship.

We reached out to a lot of these people, and the number one thing they were saying was that they wanted to use their skills to make a difference and were tired of just creating apps or software that didn't make a difference. They felt like they wanted an opportunity to give back using their skills and passion for technology rather than just doing community clean-ups or picking up trash.

Which left us with this big, latent demand out there. It was up to us to figure out how we could tap into that and how we could integrate them with a program that met that demand. A lot of the initial work with the Brigade was trying to harness the energy that came out of the Fellowship program.

TLB: So you were literally playing catch up with The Brigade?
Yeah, exactly.

And it wasn't an overnight success. We had to experiment and learn from trial and error to get it up and running. It took us a good six to seven months into the first year to really catch up in terms of having activities that people cared about, they wanted to participate in, and were passionate about.

TLB: Tell us more about what you did to learn about how to build that relationship with your audience.

The Brigade started with lots and lots of expectation from people wanting to get involved and we had to work hard to catch up to that expectation. The challenge wasn't so much about awareness, but it was about lining up our audience's expectations, our brand, and the program. We had to really ask ourselves questions like, "What is the product? What are the things that people are actually going to do? Who exactly was it for? Do we control it or is it localized? Does it need to be a social network or not?"

One of the things we've had to learn, especially in the Brigade, is how to give people the autonomy that they want and they need to create their individual identities in their community while making them part of the Code for America family and organization. We had to figure out how to balance that successfully.

One of the things we tried was to give all of our Brigade Captains @codeforamerica.org email addresses so that they have some authority, feel that they are a part of this organization, and feel empowered to do the work that they do. In doing that, we've learned that people feel like they have both the autonomy to do what they want to do but also feel really connected to us and that we care about them and they care about us. It's about respecting them and creating that sense of belonging.

That balance between autonomy and the larger connection to Code For America is really important and tells us a lot about how we scale and add as many people as possible and as many chapters as possible without us being the bottleneck. It's about figuring out what's the right balance of structure with the kind of autonomy and organic nature of the local community.

TLB: It seems like it comes down to trust. People trust that you will respect the work they want to do in their specific community, but they also trust the larger organization on the whole.

Absolutely. Trust is the first thing that we have to establish with everybody. We had to earn our credibility because people all around the country were already trying to solve these problems that the Brigade was trying to address. We were just bringing it to a national level. A huge part of that is providing value into what they're already doing.

When you think about community management—in the startup world—that's essentially the work that you're trying to have your community "brand ambassadors" do. To try and help users feel like they're part of the organization. But we wish more startups would think about that role not so much in terms of community management, but in terms of community organizing. Those people are not just your users, but they are your "people." How do you learn what empowers them? How do you harness the capacity of your audience to help push your organization in the best possible direction?

For example, some Brigades take on our identity (in terms of our logo, colors, etc.) 100% while others have a very different identity and might just sort of tag Code For America on their byline. It might surprise you, but we think that's awesome. In our case, our goal is not profit. It's that we're pushing forward with our goals within local government. If someone decides that their logo is going to look different than ours, at the end of the day, as long as their pushing forward our values and our goals, it doesn't matter if they look exactly the same as us or not.

You're not really trying to ask them to follow you as much as you are setting an example and giving them the tools so that that they can push in the direction you want them to push.

TLB: That's a powerful idea—community organizing rather than community managing. What advice would you have for other organizations that are trying to grow their audience?

Don't try to centralize control too much. We work on the Internet and are really native to Internet organizing structures. The way these stories become powerful is through decentralization. It's funny how many people who work in Internet companies try to centralize control even when they're building networked organizations. But what's most important is making people feel like they are a part of you. We really have worked, through trial and error, to make people feel like they are a part of us, a part of our growth story, and that's what has been the biggest aspect of our growth.

PART IV
LEARN:
CONTINUOUS
ITERATION

EVERYONE

SOME

FEW

← START HERE

ONE

CHAPTER 10

START LEAN, GROW LEAN

THE GROWTH, FALL, AND COMEBACK OF NETFLIX

In 1997, amidst the backdrop of movies moving from VHS to DVD, a little startup called Netflix began to challenge the titans of the entertainment industry. At the time, Netflix entered a very well-known market with a very disruptive offering—unlimited DVDs delivered to your doorstep for one low monthly fee with no late fees. They started small and found traction with an audience of passionate advocates that were fed up with the established norms and rallied behind Netflix.

From a brand development viewpoint, Netflix nailed it. Their story of unlimited freedom in entertainment choices was compelling, the wonderful artifact in their red envelope left a lasting impression, and their invitation to join them on the forefront of entertainment technology was convincing. In a few short years, Netflix became the fastest-growing first-class mail customer of the United States Postal Service and the biggest source of streaming Web traffic in North America during peak evening hours.[53] Their growth momentum was unstoppable.

In the spring of 2011, everything changed.

In a now infamous stumble, Netflix announced a pricing change through the introduction of their new brand, Qwikster. Qwikster was to handle its DVD-by-mail and Netflix its Internet streaming; offering two separate plans, websites, and cost structures. The change equated to an almost 60% price increase for customers who used both delivery methods.

The reaction was immediate: 800,000 subscribers left, Netflix's stock price dropped 77 percent in four months, and management's reputation was battered. CEO Reed Hastings went from Fortune Magazine's "Businessperson of the Year" to the target of Saturday Night Live satire. Why? Netflix violated the relationship they had built with their audience in their business attempt to grow. They took the one aspect of its service that, in their customer's mind, set them apart from its competitors and eliminated it.

With stock prices falling and customers abandoning ship, Netflix was faced with a clear choice—to stay true to its strategy or to listen to their customers and reverse course. Reed Hastings took to his blog and issued an apology:

> "I messed up. I owe everyone an explanation.
>
> It is clear from the feedback over the past two months that many members felt we lacked respect and humility in the way we announced the separation of DVD and streaming, and the price changes. That was certainly not our intent, and I offer my sincere apology. I'll try to explain how this happened."

A few weeks later, Qwikster was eliminated.

To their credit, Netflix chose to reverse course and worked to regain the trust and passion of its audience by listening to what they had to say and responding. And it worked, evident in their steady growth in both users and stock price since the infamous stumble. In fact, Netflix continues to show just how lock-and-step they are with their audience in the production of original content like *House of Cards* and *Orange Is The New*

Black—releasing full seasons at a time (a decision based on user behavior deemed "Binge-watching").

Gaining the trust of your audience is a powerful thing. If you treat your customers as something more than customers, as Netflix did during their early years, customers will respond in kind. But once you start thinking only of the bottom line, so do they.

The Netflix story is unique in that it is an object lesson in both the right way to grow and in the damage that corporate hubris can do in today's age of consumer empowerment to growth. Although Netflix stumbled, a stumble can be quickly forgotten. What will likely not be forgotten is the way Netflix—and particularly Reed Hastings—handled the stumble.

As you grow, you must grow in a way that protects your relationship with your audience by continuing to listen, engage, and respect them. Once you've found a fit with an audience, you must work to *grow your audience, grow your reach*, and *grow your culture* in a way that keeps you lock-and-step with your audience.

PRODUCT-MARKET-BRAND FIT

Let's start with finding your fit. A lot has been written about product-market fit. As venture capitalist Marc Andreessen wrote, "the only thing that matters is getting to product-market fit." At its core, product-market fit means finding a fit between the needs present, the size of the market for growth, and a product that can fulfill those needs sufficiently.

It's important to note that product-market fit represents the point at which the right product has met the right market based on the market saying so, not because the founder has. The reality is most startups fail before they ever reach true product-market fit. Although there is a ton of benefit in thinking about the development of any startup endeavor in terms of product-market fit, product-market fit alone does not take into account the impact the relationship an organization develops with its audience has. It's this relationship that will ultimately provide the startup's engine of growth.

Yes, product is vitally important. And yes, you have no business without finding a market. Without them, you're a non-started startup. But it is also true that you haven't yet validated the entire value-creation hypothesis without including the other elements of your business, collectively known as your brand.

Remember, you're inviting people to join, co-create, and invest in a relationship with you. That means product is only a part of the fit you need to find. You also can't successfully position your startup within the market without understanding how the audience will relate to the entire value offering of both product and brand. Without understanding how your brand fits into the product-market equation, you'll leave an entire avenue for value creation (emotional-value) virtually untouched and unexplored. To include the relationship you're building with your audience, you must expand your understanding of product-market fit to include brand.

Product–Market–Brand Fit (PMBF) means not only do you know how the product fits within a certain market (function-value), but you also know how the relationship your startup is generating for that market is creating value (emotional-value).

It means you have validated the emotional-value your intentional branding efforts are creating for an audience large enough to build the business you envision, you've found a way to tell your story, built artifacts that are most effective in projecting that story, and formed invitations that inspire people to join you. In an ideal scenario, finding product-market-brand fit will be a convergence wherein both product and brand are validated relatively close to one another in time.

Scale requires both. The temptation will be to scale too early. If you do, you run the risk of having to play catch up with one piece while in the process of trying to scale the other or, more likely, attempting to scale, but failing for unknown reasons.

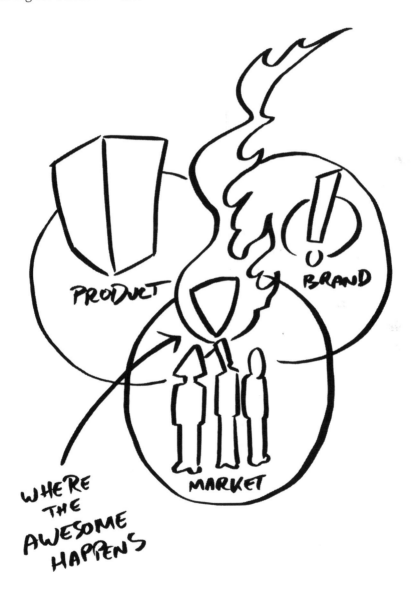

Before a startup finds Product-Market-Brand fit, nearly everything it should be doing is about discovering and learning Product-Market-Brand fit. This means learning as much as you possibly can about why people connect with you, what job they may hire your product to complete, and whether or not people are willing to cross the penny gap and join you. Pre Product-Market-Brand fit, you have to move your MVB around the Build-Measure-Learn loop until you discover the emotional-value you are creating. Post Product-Market-Brand fit you're ready to transition from a Minimum Viable Brand to a validated *brand platform*. Your brand platform is based on the learnings you've gained through experimentation in the Build-Measure-Learn feedback loop and becomes the infrastructure to support the growth of your emotional-value delivery.

Recalling the Value Stream, all of the activities in your proposed value stream are aimed at learning about how you can take a customer from first being aware to being passionate about you. All of this is in an effort to find Product-Market-Brand fit. Think about your startup in two acts: Pre Product-Market-Brand (Pre-PMBF) fit and Post Product-Market-Brand fit (Post-PMBF).

Pre-PMBF, find PMBF. Post-PMBF, scale.

GROWTH HYPOTHESIS

Once a startup finds Product-Market-Brand fit they move their learning focus from their value hypothesis to their *growth hypothesis*. Whereas a value hypothesis is an attempt to articulate the key assumption that underlies why a customer is likely to relate to your organization, a growth hypothesis represents your best thinking about how you can grow new relationships. In other words, how will new segments, markets, and audiences find your product and ultimately receive value from your organization?

On the product side, your growth hypothesis often includes production, distribution, infrastructure, IT, strategic partners and so on. On the brand side, your hypothesis often requires developing new audiences, expanding your story, evolving channels, scaling artifacts, and so on.

Growth will more than likely come from one of three "growth engines"—*organic growth* (discovering business opportunities—including business diversification—to help you grow your business slowly and opportunistically); *viral growth* (one passionate user leads to two passionate users, two begets four and so on); and *paid growth* (sustainable acquisition efforts wherein the cost of one new customer is less than the lifetime value of gaining that customer or through mergers, acquisitions, and partnerships).

No matter which engine your growth comes from, your intentional branding efforts will have a significant impact on the sustainability and scope of your growth.

In a brand context, your growth hypothesis must include your best thinking about both *external growth* and *internal growth*. The difference is important: external growth is about your audience; internal growth is about your team. Your brand plays a significant role in both.

GROWING YOUR AUDIENCE

Almost always, new customers come from the passion and evangelism of past customers. Remember, marketing can only amplify your brand, it can't create it. The old "word of mouth is your best marketing" adage still rings true.

If you've been able to develop a passionate audience around your value offering, the people who are most passionate about you should become active evangelists for your cause. Marketing isn't creating buzz, marketing is amplifying buzz that's already there.

There are certainly different nuances to what an active evangelist means for different types of business models or different types of growth engines. A B2B audience is different than a networks effect business. The key is to be able to identify your most passionate advocates in your specific business scenario.

The people who initially rallied around your startup and became passionate evangelists about you are there because you stand for something. Which means, to grow your audience the most critical ingredient is focus. The startups that win, whether a clothing company or an accounting app, are able to grow themselves through laser like focus rather than scattered attempts to appeal to the hordes.

To do this, you must remain boldly focused around the story you've articulated and validated in the market. The temptation, as you grow, add new customers, and expand your reach is to slip into "all things for all people" thinking. Don't! The more universal you try to become, the more diluted and foggy you'll be to not only your existing audience, but to potential customers as well.

To grow, focus on what's essential for continuing to build relationships with your customers first. Focus on what you learned in your MVB experimentation. And focus on building from what you know empirically worked.

Remember, a startup's job is to learn first, and then execute. The more you continue learning about your customers and how they relate to you, the more new best practices will reveal themselves, and they may or may not jive with what the experts suggest. To stay relevant, every story unfolds, evolves, and adds depth over time. The difference between evolving and attempting to become "all things to all people" comes down to remaining focused on who you are, what you stand for, and what value you are creating for your market. Don't blindly apply the latest "top 10 tips" without understanding how they fit into what you want to accomplish.

Take Amazon for example. On the surface, Amazon may appear to be unfocused as they offer everything from books to car tires. But beneath the surface is an intensely focused growth story. Amazon's growth was fostered from its ability to focus on who they are and why they matter to their audience.

Amazon found initial product-market-brand-fit with book lovers. More specifically, they found a fit with book lovers who were open to emerging e-commerce platforms like AuctionWeb (eventually eBay) and NetMarket. Amazon, at an early stage, was pushing the limits of what e-commerce could mean in today's increasingly digital world.

Their first intentional branding came in a press release in 1995:

"Amazon.com operates from headquarters in Seattle. The company maintains a staff of programmers, editors, executives, and all-around book lovers."

Not exactly the most compelling invitation: join us because we hire people who enjoy reading books. But it stuck a chord with a specific and passionate audience. A mere two years later they could credibly call themselves "earth's biggest bookstore" eventually leading to its IPO. Even when flush with capital, Amazon stayed focused on aligning its intentional branding with the reality of where they started and what it delivered to customers.

Although today Amazon is the largest online retailer in the world, their story is still focused. Amazon continues to tell a story about the technological advancement of the retail experience, whether buying books or buying tires.

CEO Jeff Bezos recently talked about Amazon's focused growth saying, "It is by design that technological innovation drives the growth of

Amazon.com to offer customers more types of products, more conve-
niently, and at even lower prices. Among its many technological innovations for customers, Amazon.com offers a personalized shopping experience for each customer, book discovery through "Search Inside The Book,"
convenient checkout using "1-Click® Shopping," and several community
features like Wish Lists that help customers discover new products and
make informed buying decisions."[54]

Amazon has remained disciplined in ensuring their branding; at any
given point in time, is never too far ahead of the reality of the value they
deliver. Although today they aren't just about books, their initial story
about evolving the retail experience through technology still rings true.
When the gulf between a brand, a product, and a market grows too far
from reality, the value of any organization is at risk.

The greatest advantage you have as a startup is your ability to focus.
Don't trade focus for short-term growth or temporary gain. In the long
run, your focus will be your best asset when it comes to growing your
brand.

Or as everyone's favorite coffee loving, bacon eating, robotic dinosaur,
FAKEGRIMLOCK, phrased it,

*"PERSONALITY = INTERESTING = CARE = TALK =
EVERYONE CARE AND TALK = YOU WIN!"*[55]

To grow an audience, the most critical aspect of your intentional branding effort is focus. Work to continually optimize your value stream from
the inside out to remain as focused as you can on providing value to your
growing audience. Although you will more than likely have to "re-brand"
or evolve your branding once the relationship has been firmly established,

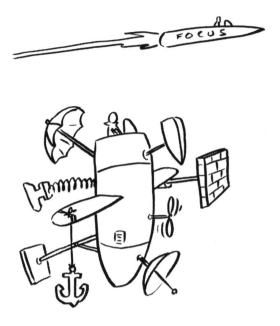

re-branding should never move you away from your core. Instead, re-branding should be about "growing" the brand so that story can include more people, extend into new markets, and sustain the core relationship you've established with early adopters.

Unfocused brand growth acts like a chameleon, attempting to change shape, size, and color with every ebb or flow of the market. Focused brand growth acts inclusively, including more and more people into who you are, what you stand for, and why you matter. Focus on who you are. Focus on who you're talking to. Focus on the synchronization between both to continually create passionate customers.

To grow your audience, be focused, don't try to be a chameleon.

CASE STUDY

DWIGHT SCHRUTE, SPIRITUALITY, AND SOULPANCAKE: GROWING YOUR STORY, AND GROWING IT WELL

An Interview With Shabnam Mogharabi (Co-Owner & CEO)

SoulPancake is challenging people to "Chew on Life's Big Questions." They've written a book, produced multiple television series, have built one of the most watched channels on YouTube—all while telling a consistent, incredible story. If you've ever seen an episode of, "Kid President," you have SoulPancake to thank. From their start, they have been telling a story that is resonating with people around the globe. Shabnam Mogharabi, Co-Owner and CEO of SoulPancake, shares their story, how they built and grew their audience, and what she believes SoulPancake has come to stand for in their audience's mind

TLB: Tell us what this whole SoulPancake thing is all about.

Ah, so what is SoulPancake? We were founded about five years ago. The company was founded by Rainn Wilson, who is the actor who played Dwight Schrute on the American version of The Office and a small group of us. At the time, he was kind of getting famous for this role that he was playing and he has always been kind of a philosophical, artistic spirit. He really felt like there was nothing online where people could have meaningful conversations. There was a lot of crap out there online and he really felt like there needed to be a place where people can have meaningful conversations.

So we decided to launch this company, SoulPancake, and the tagline we launched with was, "Chew On Life's Big Questions." We all thought this was going to be our passion project. The whole mission of the company was to get people to engage in meaningful conversations and to figure out what it means to be active participants in their human experiences and to talk about the things that we don't normally talk about.

TLB: That sounds awesome. Take us through some of that growth story.

We timed the launch of the website in March when Rainn was going to be on Oprah's "Soul Series" show. We wanted to make sure that we had the website up at that time so we were building all this content and started working on the backend developing the website and technology and all of that.

We had this one little portion of the website on the right hand side that was empty. We said, "What are we going to do with this space over here?" We decided, why don't we make that an area where people could submit their own questions? So we called it the "Question Collective." Our thinking was that we could dictate the voice and tone with our main feed with our questions and our content, but we'll give people space where they can post their own questions.

Within the first twenty-four hours after Rainn's interview, we had a surge of traffic and far and away more than three quarters of the users were posting in the "Question Collective" and not necessarily responding to the questions we had posted.

That was a really interesting thing because the users who dove into the "Question Collective" and started asking their own questions really were the people who became our core audience.

TLB: And you followed that pull?

Absolutely. We responded to it. We immediately made the "Question Collective" a larger part of the site and brought that more front and center. Everything was then collectively consumed so questions from the users as well as the questions we were putting out there to set the tone were all intermingled. We immediately realized that if this is what people want, give it to them.

TLB: From that core premise, you've been able to publish a book, been on Oprah, and have produced some amazing video. How did that happen for you?

After we launched soulpancake.com, about a year and a half later we published the SoulPancake book. And that really showed us we could take the SoulPancake mission, ethos, aesthetic, and voice that we built and turn it into content on another platform. So that was the really big move for us to take it to outside of this website we had built. Oprah Winfrey saw the SoulPancake book and loved it. She was about to launch her brand new network on television and said, "I love what you guys are doing. Can you make me some short videos that I can air on my network that feel like this book?"

We obviously said, "Yes," and that was really when we launched the production arm of SoulPancake. In the last three years we've evolved into a production media company and I think our mission has shifted a little bit. We still definitely encourage people to chew on life's big questions and figure out their human experiences, but more than anything I think our goal and our mission as a company has become to create content that uplifts and inspires people and that's thought provoking and artistic without being cheesy.

More than anything, we feel like everybody wants to feel joy and everybody wants to feel inspired, but nobody wants to feel like they're getting force-fed inspirational content. And that's where we kind of found our sweet spot. We make content that gets you to think, that opens your heart, and that makes you feel uplifted, but you don't feel like an idiot for feeling that way.

TLB: It sounds like you have a strong focus on your WHY which is informing this rallying point around inspiring people to think and engage in that portion of their life. What do you think you stand for in your audience's minds?

Joy. It's just the power of joy and the importance of joy in our lives because no one wants to not feel joyful. No one says, oh I don't want to feel joyful or I don't want to feel uplifted. Everyone wants to feel joy and everyone wants to feel that spark inside of them.

I think what has happened—especially in the last five to ten years—is we've become a very cynical and apathetic society. It became cool at some point to not care and I think joy and positivity is almost counter-culture today to what society has become. I think what our audience sees in us, as a creator of content and messages that are uplifting and unapologetically feel good, is a voice. We often say that we are inspiring a joyful rebellion and that's true, that's kind of what we are trying to do.

We do it in a very fun, irreverent, and tasteful way where you don't feel like its cheesy. But we are unapologetic about the fact that if you are going to watch our content you are going to feel good, you are going to feel joy, and you are going to open your heart—and that's okay.

TLB: A "joyful rebellion." That's great. And a passionate, strong core community has developed around that idea of joy. Why do you think this is resonating so much?

I think there are two reasons. I think the first reason is our voice. We don't take ourselves too seriously and everything we do is very respectful, but still has a level of irreverence and humor and fun in it. People responded in a way by saying, "oh this could be cool, it could be cool to talk about this. I think people really responded to our voice and our aesthetic and the way we approach what we create.

The second thing is when we were launching we were also simultaneously trying to understand who the audience was going to be. One thing we kept reading about was that a large portion of the under thirty-five crowd describe themselves as spiritual, not religious.

These were people who in our minds were on a journey to figure out who they were, what their purpose in life was, and what kind of meaning they could find in life. They didn't ascribe to a religious paradigm or a particular philosophical route or an existential route. They basically said, "I'm searching for meaning and there's something spiritual about me and I don't know what that is."

We wanted to serve that audience that was searching for meaning and looking for purpose. And we wanted to give them a place where they can ask their questions but we weren't giving them any answers. You come to the answers on your own based on all the conversations you're participating in and all the points of inspiration we are giving you and the dialogue that's created here. But you come to the conclusions after you ask the questions that are pressing for you.

TLB: So it comes back to the relationship, right? The trust, respect, and willingness to participate in these types of conversations. That really gets to the heart of what a brand really is—the relationship.

I just completely agree with that and I've seen that in every platform we've been on. Relationships are two ways, and our audience would speak to us and we would speak to them and we've always been very adamant about making sure there's two way communication between our audience and us.

But more than that I feel that like our audience really took ownership of that relationship. On our website, they took authorship over the content which helped them feel like they were owners of this brand. They were the SoulPancake community. The same with our book. People took the book and as we were building curriculum out of it, they were doing meet ups and having book clubs and college campus clubs and kind of made it their own experience. We've seen the same thing with our YouTube channel where people want to be involved and they want to be kind of ambassadors for SoulPancake.

It's been amazing to watch because it's turned into action. They've taken action for us. Like when we announced we were making a TV show, they felt like they got their own TV show. So it's amazing to just see how invested they are, so I 100% believe that!

TLB: How do you know what is working? How do you test and measure what is working in helping people become passionate advocates versus how do you know if it's not working?

The beauty of YouTube is that we can look at the analytics with a very robust backend. We can see where users are coming from, we can see how engaged they are with the content, we can see what they're sharing or what they're not sharing. Because of that we are able to see whether or not they're staying or whether they're sharing or if they're going to other content of ours. We just follow the little breadcrumbs.

I think the reason why they are getting involved is because we then take it a step further of not just listening to their comments, but we also listen to what they're asking from us.

TLB: Really practicing the art of message pull.

Right. If you give them what they want, they come out and support you and amazing things can happen. For example, we did a series called "My Last Days" that profiled people, some of them, very young, with terminal illnesses. It's a very heavy topic if you think about it. These are young people who have been told they have a terminal illness, but the way we approach it is actually very joyful and uplifting because we knew this is a show about living, it was just told by people who are dying.

So we created these eight episodes that are very uplifting and are really about how people change and embrace life based on the fact they know when they are going to die. The eighth episode was about a teenager named Zach Sobiech. He was seventeen years old and was diagnosed with osteosarcoma and been given about six months left to live from his doctors. Zach was a musician, so he was trying to say goodbye to his family by playing music. We made an episode and put it up on YouTube and it got a crazy number of views, eleven million (now over 12.5 million) or so.

There were some amazing comments, but we noticed about half of them were about, "How can I help Zach? He shouldn't be dying, and what can we do to stop osteosarcoma and get more research funded?" People were commenting about wanting to help. So we knew we shouldn't just stop the conversation there. We had eleven million people who have seen this who commented and who would want to somehow be involved. So we created the opportunity for people to do that.

We did a follow-up video and asked our audience and family and friends as well as celebrities who had tweeted about the video to send clips of them lip-syncing to a song of Zach's called, "Clouds." We collected all of these videos and put together a crowdsourced lip synching video of all these people singing to Zach's song and we just said, if you want to help Zach, donate to the osteosarcoma fund. To date, Zach has raised $750,000 for osteosarcoma research as a result of his song. What we learned is that if your audience asks for something and shows they are passionate about something, you can turn that into action.

TLB: Incredible story and amazing proof of what type of impact a passionate audience can have.

Yeah. It really showed that if you listen to your audience, if you hear what they are asking for, if you give them what they want, they come out and they will support you. It was really amazing for us to see what happened when we went beyond just looking at the analytics.

TLB: One last question. You've had some amazing support starting with Rainn and Oprah and having access to these types of celebrities. But just because you have these things doesn't presuppose that it's going to work. You've turned it into something with real value. What advice would you have for other startups about building the type of relationship you built with your audience with their potential audiences?

My advice would be, number one, listen, listen, listen to what your audience wants. More than anything, what we've learned with SoulPancake is to listen. It's why we immediately shifted to the "Question Collective" when we launched the website. It's why we put the follow-up video to Zach's story. It's why we have been able to take key content to platforms outside of YouTube. It's all because our audience is telling us what they want and we are responding to it. There is nothing more valuable than listening to what your audience wants.

To follow that up, you have to be able to pivot and change and adjust your strategy when you get that feedback. You can't be so attached to, "this is the way our company was going to be . . ." that you aren't willing to change. If you can't change and be nimble and respond to what your audience wants then you're going to become obsolete really fast.

Second, I think you have to balance the feedback from your audience with your point of view—your mission. You have to make sure when you do changes and when you listen to your audience, you always filter through the lens of what you stand for.

So our mission is to make content that is thought provoking, creative, and joyful. All of those things are the lens that we look at everything through, and if it doesn't have to do with that, we are not going to do it. So even if we shift to a "Question Collective" or we make a follow-up video or we respond to our audience when they are saying they're wanting different platforms, we do it in a way that aligns with our mission. What you stand for has to come first because that's the voice people are drawn to.

GROWING YOUR REACH

Recall the innovation spectrum. As you begin to find fit with your market you are sliding down the continuum from the disruptive side toward sustaining. The farther you go, the more traditional the branding activities become. Byron Sharp, in his book, *How Brands Grow*, framed this type of growth in terms of availability—availability of mind and availability in the store.[56] He proposes two keys to growth—wide distribution (physical availability) and distinctive memory structures (artifacts).

Physical availability refers to the spatial distance between you and your customers. Although the Internet theoretically all but dissipates the distance between an organization and a customer, a "come to me" strategy always falls short. People are over-messaged and have too many choices for you to simply throw up a website and expect people to show up.

Instead, you must go to them. Ask yourself, in both a digital and physical sense, where do our potential new customers hang out? Where are their "watering holes?" How do they prefer to be talked to? How can we best show up in their world? If you're trying to sell snow boots in Death Valley in the middle of August, it doesn't matter how great your billboard is or how amazing your story may be—you aren't in the right place.

Show up where your customers show up and intentionally expand your invitation list by meeting people where they are and working to evolve and grow your reach. The most successful growth occurs when you become "top of mind" for your market in your category.

For example, when I say, "internet search," you say _____. When I say, "online retailer," you say _____. When I say, "fast food," you say _____. (Google, Amazon, McDonald's). These three companies are undeniably top of mind. As you grow, becoming top of mind from your customer's perspective isn't an easy task, but not impossible. When I say, "online file sharing," you more than likely say, Dropbox (founded in 2008).

Think about the word or phrase you want to "own" in your audience's mind. Chances are at least one word or phrase emerged in your initial work with your MVB. To scale successfully, you must continue to build, test, iterate, and learn about the best way to solidify that word into a long standing "memory structure" with your audience. Your choices about new artifacts and invitations will directly affect the memories your customers form about you. Great memory structures are extremely clear and easily able to extend.

GROWING YOUR CULTURE

Inside of your building, it's about growing your team—attracting top talent, transitioning existing employees from innovation to execution, and building a passionate, motivated, and talented group of people around your value offering.

This is *culture.*

Culture is a building block of intentional branding and your brand's growth. Culture is the way an organization relates to itself. How do employees talk to one another? How do they collaborate? What do they value as a group? How do they get things done? From the brand perspective, it's the relationship employees—from the CEO to the delivery truck driver—form with the organization.

As the need for new team members grows, so does the need to focus on fostering internal emotional-value. A growing startup asks a lot from its employees; not only in terms of time, resources, skill, flexibility, and growth, but also in opportunity costs. For an employee, the opportunity cost of working for a startup versus working for an established company can be great; stable income vs. variable income, 9 to 5 versus all the time, and job security versus job evaporation. The risks are real for your employees and present you with a gap between landing the best people and losing them to an offer you just can't compete with.

Usually co-founders and VC's at growing startups attempt to close the gap between an employee's potential market worth and what they will make at a growing startup by offering vested and unvested stock options, preferred investment opportunities, scalable performance rewards, or other sorts of financial fringe benefits.

There is nothing inherently wrong with this approach, but promised rewards don't often do enough to push top talent over the line to join your team. After all, for smart employees, the stats on success rates in startup ventures tell them their chances of ever receiving any payoff for the risk are pretty slim.

Yet, salary and stock can be valuable incentives. In fact, throughout the 20th century, business leaders and companies alike operated as if these elements were the only incentive that mattered. They believed that if you wanted to entice the best workers, you had to pay them more. But the 21st century workplace is operating from a different set of rules. No longer are salary, stock, or future financial incentives the only variables for employees to join an organization.

Instead, as the workplace evolves and adapts in our modern context, factors like culture, values, and social impact are important in attracting the most talented people to your organization. These factors are also inherent in your brand. This means you must work to create a desire for both existing employees and future employees to join your story and remain a part of it.

Employees, just like customers, want to be a part of something they believe in and understand. They want to join something that helps them reach their personal aspirations. They want to work towards a larger vision. And not every skilled coder or star marketer will fit within the organization you're trying to build. That's why the most important aspect of your intentional branding in regards to culture growth comes back to focusing your efforts around the story you are projecting to the world.

To land top tier talent and convince them to take a risk on working for your startup, you need to build a culture within your company first that clearly stands for something and gives voice to your rallying point for your employees.

Tony Hsieh, the architect of the revered culture inside of Zappos, talked about his approach this way, "we decided to invest our time, money, and resources into three key areas: customer service (which would build our

brand and drive word of mouth), culture (which would lead to the formation of our core values), and employee training and development (which would eventually lead to the creation of our Pipeline Team). Even today, our belief is that our Brand, our Culture, and our Pipeline are the only competitive advantages that we will have in the long run. Everything else can and will eventually be copied."[57]

Remember, Hsieh isn't trying to sell shoes—he is trying to sell happiness. Think about how silly that statement is because of how high the bar is for achieving it. Not only is it what Hsieh says, it's what they do as well. Zappos is fanatical about preaching and delivering on this message both externally and internally. People want to work for Zappos. People love working there. And their culture growth has been a model for businesses large and small.

Zappos has shown the power that an internal story can have. How strongly you can articulate your story both internally and externally influences your ability to scale. Which one would you work for: a boring online store trying to sell you shoes, or Zappos who is selling happiness?

Just like your customers have a say in whether or not your product is high quality, whether or not they connect with you, and whether or not they are willing to invest their time, money, and energy into a relationship with you; employees have a say in whether your culture is good. A friend worked at a company that had a very family friendly culture. He didn't attribute that to any particular policy or initiative that made the company family friendly, it was just an underlying understanding that family life was important.

When he moved companies a few years ago, he found the culture in his new company to be completely the opposite despite the fact his new company had opened a free daycare in the office, had specific policies in place to encourage family life, and called themselves "family friendly." All of these initiatives did nothing to make their culture more family friendly as managers looked down on people who visited their kids during the day. There is no quick-fix initiative or surface level policy you can implement to manufacture culture. It's a deeply social element of your organization built upon the founders values and that develops with the people they choose to employ.

For an early stage startup, where typically a team of 3–10 comprises the entirety of the company culture, it's tough to find your bearings when it comes to growth. Focus on what you have—your story—and scale from there. Give conversations about intentional branding and culture a seat at your C-level table and foster an environment where your story shows up in hallway conversations, water cooler talks, and shared moments within your organizations life.

By solidifying who you are and having your actions be congruent to it, you are much more likely to create a powerful reason for new employees to join you and current employees to stay that stretches beyond promised financial rewards.

SUSTAIN

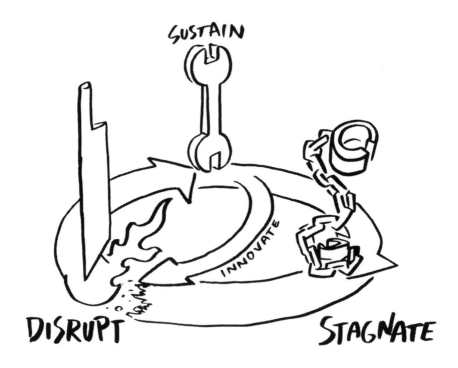

INNOVATE

DISRUPT

STAGNATE

CHAPTER 11

THE CONTINUOUS BRAND

BIG BUSINESS GETS LEAN

Technological transformation, industry disruption, depth of customer knowledge, and market savvy competition all have large enterprise executives jumpy and for good reason. Not only can competitors make major, unforeseen market penetration, but also startups and new technology can fundamentally change landscapes, seemingly overnight. We live in unprecedented times of massive uncertainty where several industries are being disrupted simultaneously. New technology in the hands of business employees and consumers alike has accelerated change.

We really don't know where we're headed. We only know the rules have changed.

Big business, as Clayton Christensen points out in his landmark work *The Innovator's Dilemma*, traditionally becomes so focused on execution; they lose the ability to innovate.[58] Lean innovation methodologies are solving this problem by giving enterprises a structure to innovate.

Not just for product development, lean innovation is rippling through other areas of the business as well, such as in sales, marketing, operations, legal teams, and UX design. Changes in the world that led to lean product innovation require change in all aspects of an organization's business model.

As lean innovation methodologies become more cemented in product innovation and sprinkled throughout the organization, the conventional branding model is proving ill-equipped to handle the new thinking. This disconnect is causing disruptions in the ability to deliver discovered value to the organization's large customer base.

Just as lean branding is transforming the approach to brand development for startups, it is being used to help larger enterprises innovate with their existing brands in several ways. First, large enterprises whose current priority is to become more agile in existing markets (in other words on the sustaining side of the innovation spectrum) use lean branding techniques to move faster, run experiments, and discover new ideas that strengthen existing relationships. Second, large enterprises undertaking initiatives to be more disruptive and achieve breakthrough innovation, use lean branding techniques that lean startups do. And finally, due to a number of different factors, well-established organizations sometimes decide to completely re-brand using lean branding techniques. This occurs in an existing market, but rather than incrementally innovate on the existing relationships, the organization decides it must radically redefine the relationships.

Brand development in these three scenarios have similarities, of course, but also fundamental differences. To implement Lean Brand techniques successfully, large or long-standing companies need four process innovations, no matter the type:

- Define your *intent to innovate*
- Invite *audience participation*
- Run *parallel innovation* between brand and product positioning
- Experiment in such a way as to *protect the core brand* and core relationships with the existing audiences.

THE INTENT TO INNOVATE

To practice brand innovation, you must start with your *intent to innovate*. Your intent to innovate focuses on where your innovation is aimed on several elements: existing market or breakthrough innovation? If existing, which elements of your brand are on the table? Are you seeking to overhaul the entire story your organization is telling? Are you making artifact changes to certain elements of your identity? In truth, you may not *know*, but have a hypothesis on where to start.

"If we change our story to x, customers will behave in ways z." Measure z, iterate.

By understanding which parts of your organization will be impacted by your innovation efforts and which will stay the same, you will be much more able to frame your hypotheses, experiments, and learnings during continuous iterative cycles of development.

Remember, planning works in reverse order: 1) figure out what you need to learn, 2) figure out how you are going to measure to know if you are gaining validated learning, and 3) figure out what you need to build to run an experiment and get a measurement.

With your intent clear, you must be willing to remove the *safety net*. When you start to get the same results, the same creative strategies, and when you're afraid to step outside of executing upon what is known—you are functioning atop a safety net.

Safety nets only tell you what *is*, not what's *possible*.

To remove the safety net *for an existing market*, it's important to routinely "break brand" to discover new insights about your emotional-value in the marketplace.

Start by asking yourself "what would happen if" or "what if" questions. "What if" our story could be communicated more concisely? "What would happen if" we changed the conversation we're having with our customers? "What if" we had more aspiration for a particular market segment?

As children, this question came quite naturally to us. "What would happen if . . . I chew on this, I ate a whole mud pie, I stand on my head for a really long time." But as we get older, this question seems to be much more messy and much more dangerous, especially in a business setting. After all, the stakes seem higher and the risk much more acute. Yet asking questions that are messy and seemingly dangerous are exactly what leads to brand innovation and ultimately real breakthrough.

Engage a small percentage of customers in a new way. Remember, insights come from direct communication with customers. Understanding the different market segments that comprise your audience will help you dive in and learn the various emotional impacts your brand is already having. Then experiment outside the existing relationship. Again, using a small subset of existing customers, and ensuring that all experiments are hypothesis driven, measure the impact of proposed brand iterations.

To break the safety net *for a new market (or breakthrough)*, you *must* experiment in the realm of messy and seemingly dangerous ideas. To work in this domain, it's best not to think of your current customers and current relationships at all. You are seeking to ask bigger questions.

Don't constrain yourself to hard and fast rules. Don't confine your thoughts to only things that have worked before. These won't get you to where you want to be, they will only tell you where you've already been. When you move away the safety net and start to explore the unknown you are transitioning from the confines of conventional branding to the opportunities of brand innovation.

The more you tend toward the breakthrough end of the spectrum, the less you can predict the ROI. Therefore, typically less money is spent

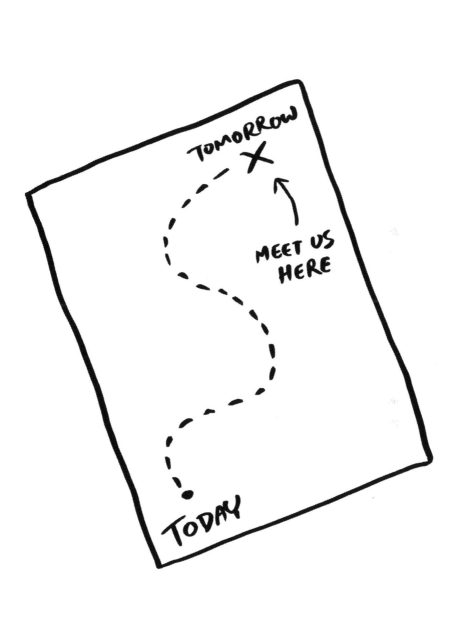

initially per breakthrough experiment, but you should be running multiple experiments. You don't *know* beforehand, which will actually "break through." Whether working in an existing market or in an unknown market, most large companies have firm return on investment (ROI) or other financial metrics and phase-gate processes that dictate how innovation should take place. Lean brand innovation plays comfortably into such structures as long as you can clearly articulate your intent to innovate.

INVITE AUDIENCE PARTICIPATION

Once your intent to innovate is clear, you must invite the participation of your audience. Launching or renovating a brand in any organization, large or small, is dependent upon audience participation. Customer feedback is vital, and companies must learn how to incorporate their audience into both their product and brand innovation efforts. You must not rely solely on subject matter experts, big data, or economic buyers. Continual customer engagement is the engine that drives validation of the evolving brand.

For an existing market, traditional means of interacting with customers work well. While you still must segment your market around shared pain or passion and not demographics, you can generally accept your customers' responses at face value. In other words, you can believe what they say.

For a new market (or breakthrough), you can't always believe what your customer has to say. They don't yet understand the context of the relationship you're exploring. This is why you want to run experiments that measure behavior, rather than relying on surveys and focus groups.

Learning to include your customers is one of the most indispensable skills an organization can have. The key is to leave behind (for the time being) your "tools of execution" when innovating. In other words, forget your surveys and focus groups and instead, have meaningful conversations with

live people so that you can understand more about them. Who are they? What drives their behavior? What impact might you have on their lives?

You may choose to invite customers to your location once a week and let your various innovation teams schedule time with them. Or you may send your teams "into the field" to facilitate connections with your audience. No matter how you ultimately engage your audience, you must invite them to participate for your innovation efforts to succeed.

PARALLEL INNOVATION

As product teams become more independent, embracing new ways of working that are optimized for speed, experimentation, and discovery, centralized branding teams are struggling to keep pace. The "command and control" paradigm of both in-house branding teams and outsourced branding agencies is coming undone in this new innovation ecosystem. Existing channels, modes of thought, and best practices are being disrupted themselves.

What's more, existing brand development methods can actually hamper the ability of an organization to use continuous innovation in other parts of the organization. If product innovation teams are dependent on a long-cycle waterfall branding process to go to market, they're doomed from the start. To sustain innovation, internal brand development teams need *parallel* ways of working to align with product teams and sustain the organizational innovation effort on the whole, while keeping their own voice involved in defining the overarching brand.

In existing markets, Lean Brand practitioners are free to experiment with components of their brand without the involvement of product development. Their ambitions should be aligned, of course, but the experiments can be separate.

In new markets, Lean Brand practitioners calibrate the workflow of both product teams and brand teams by creating one progressive flow. As product teams are building, measuring, and learning from successive minimum viable products, branding teams should be building, measuring, and learning from successive minimum viable brands. Both product and brand teams can collaborate on running experiments and integrate their tests if and when that integration makes the most sense. By uniting the work from both teams through the application of Lean Brand techniques, experimentation can work as a coordinated effort to generate as much validated learning for both teams as possible.

At the very least, brand "owners" must establish guidelines that internal lean startups can use so that they don't have to "seek permission" when running innovation experiments. Optimally, brand developers are operating on the innovation teams, offering insights, messaging, and positioning in order to enhance the experiments.

This type of *parallel innovation* effort has a significant impact on the speed and delivery of value to the customer. Instead of the long cycle times from product innovation to marketing to shelf often taking years, applying Lean Brand techniques can significantly reduce the amount of time it takes a corporation to deliver value to its customers.

PROTECTING THE CORE RELATIONSHIP

For most large organizations, the relationship between an organization and its core audience is solid. Names like Coca-Cola, Ford, GE, Nike, Kellogg's, and Budweiser are etched in the cultural fabric of our market-place. People have real and deep relationships with these companies. As we said earlier, however, that doesn't mean it will always be that way. In today's hyper-connected, social-media-frenzied world, relationships that took decades to build can be over in minutes.

Needless to say, an existing enterprise can incur significant brand risk by running experiments with their paying customers. The need to protect the core brand in the eyes of the customer is crucial.

New innovation should never put the core relationship with an audience at significant risk. Yet, almost every large company knows that it also needs to deal with ever-increasing external threats by continually innovating. The need for innovation—and the parallel inefficiencies in supporting teams like brand development—can create clear tension between innovation teams and the teams that support them.

To mitigate tension, brand managers need to be able to de-risk any potential negative impact on the core brand without quelling innovation altogether. This means recognizing the difference between executing on a known brand platform and developing a completely new one.

For high-volume product branding such as the worldwide launch of a new soda or a new model of smartphone, lean branding allows you to scale your MVB testing in multiple markets without risking the core brand. Purposeful (sustaining-side) MVB testing protects the core brand.

You must ask yourself, does our new brand align with the rest of the relationship? Does it reinforce the existing brand? Does it fit into the overall aspiration we are helping our customer achieve? If it does, then it fits within the story you're telling and can work to enhance your existing brand. If it doesn't, then perhaps it needs to be a spin-off or stand alone brand or perhaps be reevaluated to fit within the existing relationship.

For example, when Gatorade launched its new product line of before, during, and after sports drink supplements (G1, G2 & G3), it was extending and enhancing the core relationship with its audience. The new

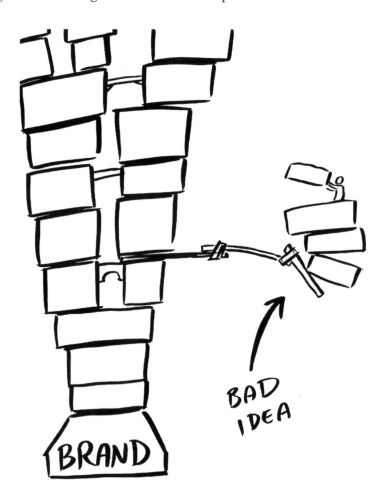

products aligned with the story Gatorade had established in helping their customers be better athletes. Yet if Gatorade were to get into the athletic wearables category, they would have to seriously experiment to learn how the new product might fit into the existing relationship.

You must continue to think of your brand as two parts: the customers' expectation at the core, and the surface elements that signal that expectation. Usually, it's less risky to get the expectation right first (through conversation and low-fi prototypes), then invest in the surface elements once the expectation, customer need, and relationship is validated. This ensures that the core relationship remains intact and helps to de-risk any experiments you may run on the innovation side.

DEVELOPING A LABS BRAND

The journey toward brand innovation will be different for every organization. Transforming existing teams inside an existing organization is often not viable. There are existing products running at scale, there is revenue and brand to protect, and there are a lot of stakeholders to get onboard. One strategy for transformation is to develop a labs extension brand of the larger business.

A labs brand is an independent business unit typically comprised of people with skills in development, product management, design, and marketing to form a core startup team. Support for the labs brand comes from access to domain expertise and feedback, access to resources, and access to existing customers. Companies like Nordstrom, Intuit, Mastercard, Wells Fargo, Intel, Qualcomm, and Ford have all taken this approach to their internal innovations.

A labs brand allows an enterprise to rapidly run experiments with products, product-branding, and brand-building within a safe-to-fail dedicated piece of the business. Lean methodologies were born in environments where ideas had to be quickly tested on customers, with little money to fund these experiments. Leveraging a labs extension within the larger organization can allow for quick, sustainable implementation of lean principles, while protecting the core-brand.

Consider the differences between Webvan, which invested $1 billion on warehouses, fleets of trucks and web infrastructure; and Zappos, which started with the most lightweight e-commerce site possible, and no inventory. Both companies were founded in 1999, yet Webvan went bankrupt two years later losing the $1 billion investors had poured in, while Zappos was acquired by Amazon in 2009 for about $1.2 billion—a great return for investors who put in about $60 million.

What did Zappos do differently? It functioned like a lean startup by building a Minimum Viable Product, Minimum Viable Brand, and quickly building relationships with customers right away, proving that its concept—selling shoes at full retail, with emphasis on great customer service—would work. In contrast, Webvan made large, sweeping investments before building strong relationships with an audience that could sustain its growth and success.

Imagine if your organization could incubate and produce a Zappos-like success. A labs extension can do just that by allowing you to begin shipping a minimally viable brand faster; embracing automated testing and continuous iteration; and implementing startup-like processes like sprints, persona mapping, and Build-Measure-Learn looped experimentation—all of these enabled by the resources and close proximity to the larger corporation on the whole.

A labs brand allows your organization to innovate like a startup without risking the entire brand all at once. It allows you to invite audience participation across multiple channels, resources, and platforms by empowering

your internal startups to have access to customers who have "adopted in" to startup experiments.

For organizations continuously releasing new products, a labs brand is parallel innovation at its best—fully integrated, contiguous innovation. Just like a startup, corporations must approach new products and product lines as opportunities to discover the value being created and for whom that value is being created.

Disney's success with *Toy Story* was almost unprecedented as critics made it the fourth best reviewed film of all time and viewers flocked to the theater in droves. No film sold more tickets in the United States in 1995. Yet, *Toy Story* wasn't made by the Walt Disney Animation Studio. At the time, little known startup Pixar was opening a new horizon with the first computer-animated feature ever and consequently forming a new relationship with an audience Disney had failed to find strong footing with—young adults.

The distribution of *Toy Story* represented a completely new product for Disney in computer-animation that was facilitated by its labs extension, Pixar. But Pixar wasn't an overnight success. They had built a strong following amongst computer-animation early adopters producing a few short films, commercials, and some 3-D shorts for Nickelodeon and Sesame Street.

RE-BRAND: LEAN AT SCALE

For organizations attempting transformation through a "re-brand" of the entire organization, the variable to applying lean brand techniques is scale. Typically, to test re-branding efforts corporations turn to big data, focus group style market research, and conventional branding agencies. Not only is big data and focus group research alone just modeled statistics in the form of trends, it isn't validated learning. But, as we've discussed at length throughout this book, the conventional model is ill equipped to handle true innovation.

Instead, implementing Lean Brand techniques comes down to the scale that the new "brand" will be used on. JCPenny, in their recent rebranding attempt, went with big data trends to try to re-brand and failed. They launched big, spent millions of dollars on surface artifacts, and failed to validate their approach with their audience. The rebirth of Gap was a different story. Their success was largely predicated on their validated learning through their partnerships with fashion blogs. In what they learned through low-level experiments with various fashion blog audiences, the Gap was able to make a significant comeback after years of dwindling earnings.

Implementing lean branding in a "re-branding" effort comes down to moving fast, building quickly, automating testing, validating your ideas through feedback, building successive MVBs, and getting as close to your audience as you can.

No matter your application of lean branding to your organization, the key is in finding ways to link *both* product innovation and brand innovation. Your audience doesn't experience your products and brand as separate entities, they experience them as one holistic value offering. Lean branding provides a powerful way to ensure your efforts on both fronts are united in their appeal and value to your audience.

Using lean branding will help you create and foster a culture that allows experimentation, embraces innovation, and is driven by validated learning. While large corporations may have an advantage in resources and capital more so than anyone else, they are met with challenges that independent startups don't have. Lean branding can help any existing branding efforts become more aligned, more accessible, and ultimately more valuable for your organization.

CHAPTER 12

THE LEAN BRAND STACK

THEORY & TOOLS, TOOLS & THEORY

There is no shortage of grand theories and tools at your fingertips to help you develop your brand. Bookshelves are crammed full of various books offering processes and ideas about brand development. Even more, the Internet is overflowing with endless best practices, devices, tricks, and pro tips. The challenge for any startup is to understand which ideas and which tools will help you build sustainable, passionate relationships with your audience.

Blindly applying DIY guides and "pro tips" to your brand development can be an expedient way to obscure your value potential. Just take a look at the "swoosh epidemic" so many logos suffered in the late 1990's or the Web 2.0 twitter imitators in 2009. For the most part, following trends leads to blasé, predictable results that won't give you much staying power in the long run.

To discover and create real value, you have to have solid footing in how you approach your brand formation (theory) and capable mechanisms to work with (tools). You must also learn to recognize the intersection between the two—both your approach and the tools you use are inextricably tied to one another.

The Lean Brand framework provides a methodology to forming the foundations for the relationships you develop with people. But the framework, just like all methodologies, is supported by tools to help it work. Throughout each chapter, there have been multiple suggestions on ways to apply and use the ideas in this book. From outside the office activities to introspective exercises, there have been multiple suggestions to help your brand-formation work move you toward success.

We've also designed a specific set of tools to help you along your Lean Brand journey. Unlike a wide reaching "brand strategy plan" that is seldom updated, takes too long to write, and is almost never actually used in the long run; these tools are designed to help you discover value with your audience.

Introducing, the *Lean Brand Stack*.

THE LEAN BRAND STACK

The Lean Brand Stack is a set of tools to help you iterate quickly, learn as much as you can, and build passionate relationships with your audience. The stack includes four primary tools for you to use in your Lean Brand efforts—*The Persona Grid*, *The Minimum Viable Brand Canvas*, *The Experiment Map*, and *The Value Stream Matrix*.

The stack will help guide you in your practical application of the ideas in this book. They are meant to be used as a resource in the hard work of developing passionate advocates for your organization and as diagnostic tools to help you understand and improve your value offering. The four tools are intentionally organized into a *stack* to guide you through successive turns of the Build-Measure-Learn feedback loop. The stack will allow you to work on brand development together with your team, your board, or anyone else who can be an asset to your efforts.

Keep in mind, the tools included in the stack are not meant to be tasks you must complete, but rather springboards for you to work from. The stack will assist you as you rapidly sketch out brand ideas, put together new experiments, and measure their results.

In all of your work, never trade the tools for the overall effect of the whole framework. The overall purpose of the Lean Brand framework is to discover the emotional-value you are creating and for whom that value is being created. There are multiple paths to this discovery. That's why you must embrace the methodology without becoming too systematic about its application. Each organization's journey will progress differently.

What's important is that every experiment you run, every iteration of your MVB, and each learning you generate should be driving you towards building a passionate audience around your value offering. In the following sections, we'll dive a bit deeper into each tool and teach you how to best use the Lean Brand Stack.

To download a digital, hi-resolution version of the Lean Brand Stack visit http://leanbrandbook.com.

THE PERSONA GRID

The *Persona Grid* is about your audience. It gives you a simple, quick way to start to summarize the information you are learning about the audience you're addressing. The grid was designed to help you understand the needs of your audience and narrow your focus using two techniques: observation and interpretation. On the left side of the grid, focus on what you can observe about your audience. Analyze their lives and work to uncover the characteristics of your persona. Use the "Looks" and "Life" boxes on the left side of the grid to gather data about the characteristics of your audience.

What do they look like?
Where do they live?
Are they married or single?
What does a typical day in his / her life look like?

On the right side of the grid, focus on what you can interpret from your audience. Use intuition and empathy to try and understand what drives your audience. Use both the "Likes" and the "Love" boxes on the right side of the grid to gather intuitive data about the character of your audience.

What is his / her aspiration?
What are their strongest beliefs?
What do they do for fun?
Who do they want to become?
What is his or her personality like?

The combination of your persona's looks, life, likes, and loves will help to center decisions surrounding your MVB by adding a layer of real-world audience consideration to the conversation. It also offers you a rapid and inexpensive way to test and prioritize your audience throughout the development process. You should use a separate grid for each type of persona you are exploring and create as many personas as you need for all the different groupings of cohorts you're working on.

For the persona grid to be most valuable, you must go out and find real people to validate that a persona actually exists. These people will become the people you are going to test and validate or invalidate your assumptions, your MVBs and MVPs, and value hypotheses with. With each new learning about your audience, come back to the persona grid and update each box with your new insight. Over time, you'll be able to see a clearer and clearer picture of your audience's preferences, aspirations, and behaviors leading to more and more valuable information for your growth.

To that end, you should routinely revisit your personas. People change whether through life experiences, exposure to new innovations, or just on

PERSONA GRID™

CAPTURE, TEST, AND UPDATE RELEVANT AUDIENCE DETAILS

PERSONA'S NAME:

L	R
TECHNIQUE: **ANALYSIS + OBSERVATION** FOCUS: **CHARACTERISTICS** GOAL: **UNCOVER**	TECHNIQUE: **INTUITION + INTERPRET** FOCUS: **CHARACTER** GOAL: **UNDERSTAND**

LOOKS
APPEARANCE

- Insert a photo or image that best represents your audience
- If possible, include an image that shows where they will use your product (work, home, play, etc.)

LIKES
PSYCHOGRAPHICS

- List common personality traits
  What do they do for fun, relaxation, or enjoyment? (activities and interests)
  What are their favorite social sites, magazines, blogs, websites, etc?
- List other relevant attitudes, values, or behaviors

LIFE
DEMOGRAPHICS

- What does a day in their life look like?
- Where do they live?
- Educational background?
- Relationship or marital status?
- Children? Pets?
- Describe current work or job environment
- Previous work experience or history?
- What are their friends like? Colleagues and co-workers?

LOVE
ASPIRATIONS

- What are their strongest beliefs and opinions?
- What do they want to achieve, improve, or make better? How do we help them?
- Who or what do they idolize? Who do they want to become? How do we help them?
- What type of experience do they want or expect? What would delight them?

a whim. Always take advantage of opportunities to get closer and closer to a real-time understanding of your audience.

THE MINIMUM VIABLE BRAND CANVAS

The *Minimum Viable Brand Canvas* is a tool you can use to dive into your MVB work. It will help you build successive iterations of your brand that enable full turns of the Build-Measure-Learn loop with a minimum amount of effort and the least amount of development time.

The canvas works as both a tool for development and as a diagnostic aid to support your intentional brand development efforts through multiple iterations.

Don't settle on your initial run through the canvas; keep working through various iterations to get the best out of the tool. Sketch out alternatives and options to compare and contrast against so you can discover the best path of development possible. Simply filling in the slices won't get you anywhere.

The MVB Canvas works best when printed out large scale or projected onto a screen so groups of people can jointly start sketching, hypothesizing, and discussing the elements. As you start to work with the canvas, we encourage you to use post-it notes for each of the ideas you have within each of the slices. Your ideas need to remain fluid, and we've found sticky-notes allow for your ideas to remain flexible rather than linear.

We also encourage you to use words and drawings, photos, or other visual representations of your ideas. Colors, shapes, pictures, doodles, and sketches are all ways to deepen your understanding of your ideas and enhance your sense of the bigger picture. Finally, it may help to keep a running collection of MVB canvases to map out new or successful brands you come across. Applying an MVB canvas to companies you admire or you want to learn from can help you understand what they did to find success.

MVB CANVAS™

BUILD, TEST, AND ITERATE YOUR MINIMUM VIABLE BRAND

VITALS

ORGANIZATION:

PERSONA SEGMENT:

DATE:

ITERATION NO:

STORY

RALLY POINT

YOUR WHY

BELIEFS / VALUES

MEDIUM

MVB

INVITATION

MESSAGE

CHANNELS

FEEL (INTERACT)

ARTIFACTS

SEE (VISUAL)

EXPERIENCE

Canvas Components

Story

Story is your story. Who you are as founders. Who you are as a startup. Why people should care about a relationship with you. This is your unique rallying point defining what you're fighting against and what you're fighting for.

Artifacts

Artifacts are projections of your story. Remember John Deere's green tractor and Corona's lime? The goal is to find artifacts that project your story and engage people with who you are. Great artifacts evoke emotion and reflect the relationship you are forming with your audience.

Invitation

Invitations are active calls for people to join you on a journey toward shared value. By sketching out what you say, where you say it, and how you say it, invitations impact the way people respond to you.

Using The Minimum Viable Brand Canvas

Start with your story. In the story slice of the canvas, using sticky notes, drawings, doodles, words, images, and anything else you have sketch out your ideas about your founder story, what you stand for as you startup, your rallying point, and what you aspire to become. Then try to narrow all of those ideas into a single, compelling story that best captures who you are. This story may be a single word, a phrase, or a few paragraphs you believe will reflect the relationship you intend to pursue with an audience. Once you have your ideas for your story on the canvas, move on to your artifacts.

In the artifact slice of the canvas, use words, images, and even samples of artifacts that you believe would best project the story you've defined on the canvas. You may want to cut out photos from magazines, paste business cards you've been collecting, or even glue the artifact itself to the canvas. Which one artifact do you believe will be most engaging for your audience? Which artifact projects your story in the most dynamic way? Which artifact is most representative of who you are becoming as an organization? This artifact is the one you'll use to test with this iteration of your MVB.

Finally, move to the invitation slice of the canvas. How will you best communicate your desire for a relationship with your audience? What should you say? How will you say it? Where will you deliver your invitation? Sketch out ideas about your tone of voice, the content you want to create, and the mediums you think will work. Use specific examples, specific channels, and specific words you think will best tell your story. Then narrow your choices down to a single, compelling invitation that you intend to test with your audience for this iteration of your MVB.

Use this iteration of your MVB to experiment with through the Build-Measure-Learn feedback loop. You'll want to measure, concisely, how each component resonates with your audience using the emotional-value metrics we discussed in Chapter 8. Did people light up with your artifact or did they ignore it? Did your story resonate, or did it fall flat? Did people choose to join you or did your invitation miss the mark? What component do you need to iterate on? Which do you need to expand?

Using your results from your first experiments, you can then start a new canvas to sketch out, hypothesize, and track the next iteration of your MVB. In this way, the MVB Canvas becomes both a tool to sketch out your ideas and a diagnostic tool, allowing you to measure the growth of your relationship with your audience through successive experiments, learnings, and iterations.

THE EXPERIMENT MAP

The *Experiment Map* is designed to help document the various experiment loops you'll experience as you search for Product-Market-Brand fit. The Experiment Map documents your journey over time, making it easy to communicate your progress to your team members, investors, advisors, and even to yourself. We've tested it with hundreds of experiments, and it works.

The Experiment Map is focused on recording experiments. It is especially helpful during workshops and events such as hackathons, boot camps, and accelerators. It can also be extremely useful for improving existing products, or in any other situation where you are using the Build-Measure-Learn loop to make rapid progress.

It is designed as a physical printed poster, on which you place sticky notes as you progress. The physical nature of a poster is valuable for a variety of reasons, providing a simple structure for your experiments and encouraging you to follow a bit more discipline as you explore new experiments.

You record content on the poster as you go down each column, which can be easily accessed later as you tell your story. Using the Experiment Map makes it easy to bring new team members up to speed fast, and provide a visible way to measure progress.

Using The Experiment Map

Begin by establishing your key "leap of faith" assumptions, then proceed to generate key hypotheses for these leaps of faith. Based on your hypothesis, you then document potential experiments to run, including

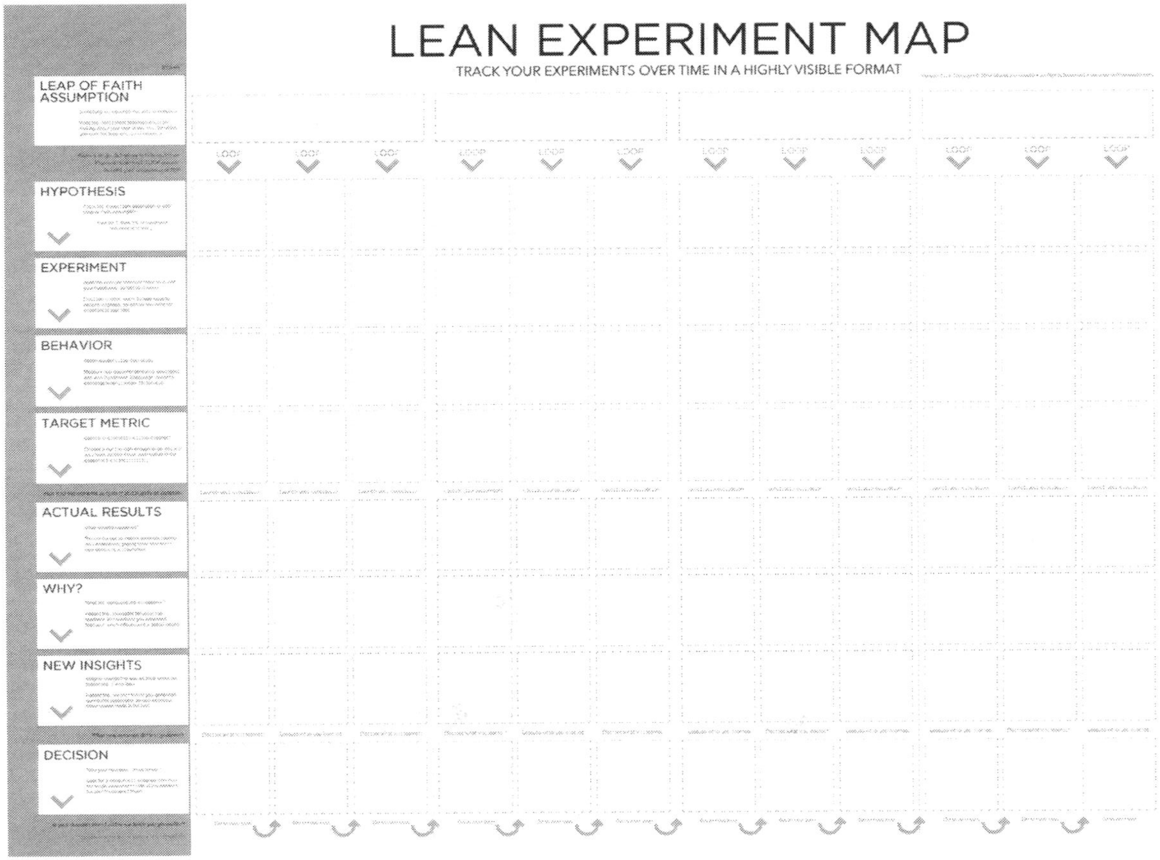

LEAN EXPERIMENT MAP

TRACK YOUR EXPERIMENTS OVER TIME IN A HIGHLY VISIBLE FORMAT

LEAP OF FAITH ASSUMPTION

HYPOTHESIS

EXPERIMENT

BEHAVIOR

TARGET METRIC

ACTUAL RESULTS

WHY?

NEW INSIGHTS

DECISION

measurable behaviors and target metrics. Once your experiment is over, be sure to record your results, as well as new learning and insights you now have. You then use this new "data" to make your next decision, and the process repeats itself. As you record each experiment, your experiment map poster creates a record of your progress.

You provide all the content on sticky notes, then place the notes in the corresponding boxes. The small size of the sticky notes forces you to be succinct in your answers, and encourages you to break problems into small component parts. Since you are able to see all experiments at once, you can quickly make connections between multiple insights, and get a true sense of your progress.

THE VALUE STREAM MATRIX

In any successful organization, a certain number of customers go through a series of steps to become passionate advocates for your business. The value stream looks at the eventual delivery of value to your customer through their eyes. They must become aware of you, be intrigued with your value offering, become trusting of you and your offer, be convinced to buy from you, become hopeful that their purchase will be worth it, be satisfied with your offering, and eventually become passionate about you and the value you provide. The **Value Stream Matrix** is a tool designed to help you define and track your value discovery efforts.

No matter what your startup endeavor is, your job is to discover the value being created, and for whom it's being created, and whether there's a large enough market to support the business you envision. Fundamental changes will occur in your thinking between your initial concepts and its actual delivery. Your early assumptions about how you develop relationships with your audience will likely be proven wrong. There is nothing wrong with that. In fact, it is the natural way that any entrepreneur learns

VALUE STREAM MATRIX

DISCOVER, TRACK, AND ITERATE YOUR VALUE STREAM

ORGANIZATION:

PERSONA SEGMENT:

DATE:

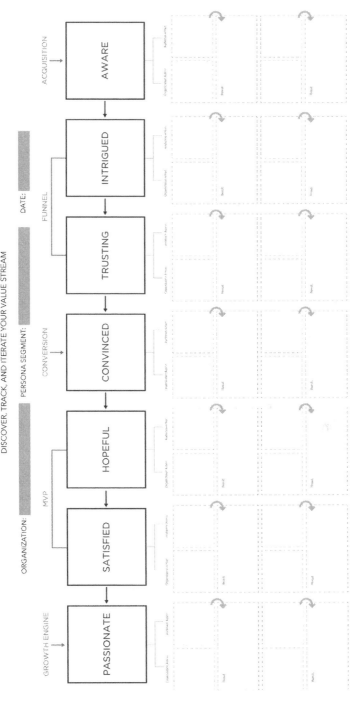

ACQUISITION — AWARE

FUNNEL — INTRIGUED — TRUSTING

CONVERSION — CONVINCED

MVP — HOPEFUL — SATISFIED

GROWTH ENGINE — PASSIONATE

how to deliver value to its audience. Your objective is to learn what is fundamental to your business success with the minimal amount of effort.

The matrix is designed to be printed as a poster, on which you can place sticky notes to keep track of your value stream discovery. For each step of the stream (aware, intrigued, trusting, convinced, hopeful, satisfied, passionate) you want your customer to move on to the next step. You want them to take a specific action to indicate that they have moved on. As a business, you must do something or have something that leads the customer to take that action. It is easy to imagine a whole list of activities a business may deploy for each stage, but the goal is to discover what is optimal.

Use the Value Stream Matrix to posit one best-case scenario and work to validate that scenario through experimentation and validation (using the experiment map). Using your ideal audience (from the persona grid) construct an "ideal" path a customer will take from first becoming aware of you to eventually becoming passionate about their relationship with you. Remember, your customer will do something to indicate they've taken a step through the stream. In other words, you want to measure the customer's action to track how they move through your value stream. Sometimes this can be done with simple analytics and in other cases, it must be much more robust. No matter the case, be sure to record your results in the Value Stream Matrix, as this will lead you to discovering the most optimized value stream possible.

THIS, NOT THAT; THAT NOT THIS

Like most things in life, lean branding is a series of continuous choices. With each choice you make, you are both articulating the relationship with your audience and, at the same time, understanding what that relationship isn't. No decision you make about your brand development is unidirectional. For instance, if you say you're a rebel, you are also saying you aren't mainstream. If you say you're blue, you are also saying you're not green, yellow, black, purple, and so on. No decision is made in a vacuum. Every decision communicates to your audience: you are this, not that; or that, not this.

Value discovery and delivery should be your lens in determining your relationship with your audience. If you don't understand how you create value, you are assured a quick trip to the valley of death. All of your decisions about your brand-formation have to be filtered through the lens of value creation. Your decisions should always take into account the relationship you are building with your customers, the vision you have for your company, the resources available to you, and the environment you are building in.

Remember, at the onset a startup's job is to learn, and as such, your decisions should always be based on the validated learning you're gaining through experimentation and iteration. Stand by what you learn and grow from it.

THE LEAN STARTUP MOVEMENT

In the past few years, the Lean Startup movement has picked up significant traction and popularity. The movement has found its way into meetups, incubators, MBA programs, large enterprises, and emerging startups around the globe. Not only is it popular, but it works. There are countless success stories from a multitude of disciplines ranging from the social impact community to the high-tech hives. The Lean Startup community is full of incredible innovators working to move our industries, ideas, and cultures forward.

The Lean Brand methodology deepens the Lean Startup movement by contributing a framework for startups to integrate brand development into the activities and ideas they're already employing as a lean startup. Whereas *The Lean Startup* and *The Lean Entrepreneur* provide a methodology and techniques to create innovative products, *The Lean Brand* focuses on developing innovative relationships. When combined, the ideas and practices expressed in *The Lean Startup*, *The Lean Entrepreneur*, and *The Lean Brand* provide a dynamic platform for innovation, creation, and value discovery in today's value-driven marketplace.

As you grow, your core advantage will remain your ability to validate your assumptions in "live" settings through the Build-Measure-Learn feedback loop. Eric Ries articulated this advantage by saying, "Lean Startups, when they grow up, are well positioned to develop operational excellence based on lean principles. They already know how to operate with discipline, develop processes that are tailor-made to their situation, and use lean techniques."

The benefits of lean thinking are immense and the community that has sprouted around its principles represents an enormous availability of resources for veteran practitioners and aspiring entrepreneurs alike. If you're already a part of the movement, cheers! If you aren't, consider this your official invitation.

THE LEAN BRAND MOVEMENT

On it's own, the Lean Brand Community is a movement of startups, growth hackers, agencies, branding practitioners, entrepreneurs, marketers, innovative executives, and organizations joining together to shift the way we think about brand development in the new value-creation economy.

In this book, we've explored a new paradigm for brand innovation. But the ideas provided are opinions meant to help reframe the way you approach your branding. Like all opinions, they may or may not work in your specific environment, scenario, set of circumstances, or market.

Branding, business models, marketing, product engineering, design, production, distribution, investments, customers, employees, markets, technology, channels, and so on, are all interconnected in the real world. There is no way to practically extract one from the group and treat it as independent from everything else and expect success.

The purpose of focusing in on your brand development is to explore the unique value potential your relationships are creating for your audience. Branding is a practice, not an asset. That's why you must think about your brand development in terms of a *continuous brand*. A continuous brand is alive, growing, moving, shaping, and evolving each and every day.

As a movement, the Lean Brand Community must avoid doctrines and rigid ideology. Beyond simply applying the Lean Brand principles to our organizations, our goal should be to change the entire ecosystem, approach, processes, and practices of branding on the whole. To do this, we must continue to learn and improve our work in Lean Brand development. This means sharing with one another the wins and losses of our development efforts. It means spurring one another on toward success and supporting one another along the journey. This is how true movements act.

A FINAL WORD: DO GOOD, FOR GOODNESS SAKE

A brand is a powerful tool to wield in the market. Businesses, corporations, startups, and so on are not people, but people comprise and create them. How the people within these organizations behave, think, feel, communicate, and act define how the business behaves on the whole. This is important to understand in light of how much brand work relies on relationships, psychology, and human emotion.

A brand should be a natural extension of the collective characteristics and personalities of the people involved. It can also become a disingenuous business strategy used to manipulate customers and target segments regardless of the emotional or human cost.

Branding—as well as all aspects of a business—must acknowledge the responsibility of *doing good*. Branding particularly, due to its emotional nature, when used for evil can be a loaded tool used to influence, bend, and exploit people in unthinkable ways. Unfortunately, there is no shortage of stories of fly-by-night organizations using branding to manipulate their customers in nefarious ways.

Inversely, when a brand is used for good, it can create incredible opportunities for positive impact in the world. Although the mishaps get the most press, there are astonishing stories of organizations using the relationships they've developed with their audience to help, guide, and benefit our world.

In the startup world, there are countless entrepreneurs focusing their brilliance on finding ways to make millions of dollars. They vet opportunities in the market by focusing on questions like, "Will people pay for this?" or "How can I 'monetize' this?" without asking, "Will this make people's lives meaningfully better?" It's not that you shouldn't try to make a profit, but profits are only part of a much larger picture of what we should strive for as the innovators, game changers, and creators that we are.

The challenge, then, is to make the hard choices to make your existence as a business a benefit for society by balancing economic performance and social value while demonstrating that it's not a zero-sum game.

In the words of Voltaire, *"Every man is guilty of all the good he did not do."*

In all things, do good.

JOIN THE LEAN BRAND COMMUNITY AT
LEANBRANDBOOK.COM

- Download your digital copy of the Lean Brand Stack
- Get artwork from the book
- Join Lean Brand practitioners from around the globe
- Stay up to date on the latest techniques, case studies and application of the framework with the Lean Brand Blog.
- Share your Lean Brand story
- Get insider news, access to global events, and stay connected by joining the Lean Brand Newsletter.

A NOTE FROM JEREMIAH & BRANT

If you're all the way back here, thank you for reading! We hope you enjoyed the book and will make it your own in your efforts to build a passionate audience. Like all new ideas, **word of mouth is crucial for success**. If you are passionate about the ideas in this book, will you take two minutes to leave a review of The Lean Brand on Amazon.com. Your thoughts are important to the continued success of these ideas. Even if your review is short, it makes a big difference.

Thank you for your support,

Jeremiah & Brant

Go to LeanBrandBook.com/amazon to leave your review.

ENDNOTES

Chapter 1

1. Paul Biedermann 17 year Creative Director for McGraw Hill and now Creative Director at re:DESIGN
2. Charlene Li and Josh Bernoff, Authors of *Groundswell*
3. American Marketing Association. See also: The MASB Common Language Project. http://www.themasb.org/common-language-project/ http://en.wikipedia.org/wiki/Brand
4. Al Ries—Author of *The 22 Immutable Laws of Branding* and *Positioning: the Battle for Your Mind*
5. Ann Handley—MarketingProfs Author with C.C. Chapman of *Content Rules*
6. David Ogilvy, Author of *Ogilvy On Advertising*
7. You can read the entire GM document here: "The 69 Words You Can't Use at GM." Corporate Intelligence RSS. 1 May 2014. Web. 15 May 2014. <http://blogs.wsj.com/corporate-intelligence/2014/05/16/the-69-words-you-cant-use-at-gm/>

Chapter 2

8. AMC'S *Mad Men*. *Mad Men*: Season One. Created by Matthew Weiner. Perf. John Hamm, Elisabeth Moss, January Jones, John Slattery, Vincent Kartheiser. Lionsgate, 2008. DVD
9. These awards are seriously called the "Brand Genius Awards." You can check them out for yourself here: http://www.adweek.com/brand-genius

10. Nilofer Merchant, *11 Rules for Creating Value in the Social Era* (Harvard Business Press Books, 2012).

11. Sir Ken Robinson, *Out of our Minds* (John Wiley & Sons, 2011).

Chapter 3

12. Ries, Eric. *The Lean Startup: How Today's Entrepreneurs Use Continuous Innovation to Create Radically Successful Businesses* (Crown Business, 2011).

13. The "Toyota Production System." Read more about TPS from the creators themselves, Toyota: http://www.toyota-global.com/company/vision_philosophy/toyota_production_system/

14. Shadow Force: a core competency, operational excellence, or key differentiator internal to the business which allows it to outperform the competition (from Cooper, Brant, and Patrick Vlaskovits. *The Lean Entrepreneur: How Visionaries Create Products, Innovate with New Ventures, and Disrupt Markets* (Wiley, 2013).

15. Simon Sinek, *Start with Why: How Great Leaders Inspire Everyone to Take Action* (Penguin, Oct, 2009).

Chapter 5

16. Gottschall, Jonathan. *The Storytelling Animal: How Stories Make Us Human* (Houghton Mifflin Harcourt, 2012).

17. Signorelli, Jim. *StoryBranding: Creating Standout Brands through the Power of Story* (Greenleaf Book Group, 2012).

18. Simon Sinek, *Start with Why: How Great Leaders Inspire Everyone to Take Action* (Penguin, 2009).

Chapter 6

19. You can read all 27 pages with some commentary here: "Pepsi Logo Design Brief: Branding Lunacy to the Max." Fast Company. Web. 4 June 2014. <http://www.fastcompany.com/1160304/pepsi-logo-design-brief-branding-lunacy-max>

20. Ferrazzi, Keith, *Who's Got Your Back: The Breakthrough Program to Build Deep, Trusting Relationships That Create Success—and Won't Let You Fail* (Broadway, 2009)

21. M, Martin, *Brand Sense: Build Powerful Brands through Touch, Taste, Smell, Sight, and Sound* (Free, 2005).

22. Do a quick Google search for "SoulPancake heart attack" and watch the video, it'll bring a smile to your face.

Chapter 7

23. *Field of Dreams*. Dir. Philip A. Robinson. Perf. Kevin Costner and James Earl Jones. Universal, 1989.

24. Brogan, Chris, and Julien Smith. *Trust Agents: Using the Web to Build Influence, Improve Reputation, and Earn Trust* (John Wiley & Sons, 2009).

25. Gene Weingarten, "Pearls Before Breakfast By Gene Weingarten," Washington Post, Sunday, April 8, 2007

26. Business Insider Intelligence. http://www.businessinsider.com/chart-of-the-day-number-of-texts-sent-2013-3

27. YouTube. "Statistics" http://www.youtube.com/yt/press/statistics.html

28. Skype. "Thanks for Making Skype a Part of Your Daily Lives—2 Billion Minutes a Day!" http://blogs.skype.com/2013/04/03/thanks-for-making-skype-a-part-of-your-daily-lives-2-billion-minutes-a-day/

29. "The Neilsen Cross-Platform Report Q4 2012." http://www.nielsen.com/us/en/newswire/2013/zero-tv-doesnt-mean-zero-video.html

30. Radicati Group Inc. "Email Statistics Report, 2012–2016," Radicati.com, April 2012. http://mashable.com/2012/11/27/email-stats-infographic/

31. Mashable. "Did You Know 144.8 Billion Emails Are Sent Every Day?" http://mashable.com/2012/11/27/email-stats-infographic/

32. Caitlin Johnson, "Cutting Through Advertising Clutter," CBSNews.com, 2006. http://www.cbsnews.com/news/cutting-through-advertising-clutter.

33. Louise Story, "Anywhere the Eye Can See, It's Likely to See an Ad," NYTimes, 2007.

34. Extensive list of the variance in the research about how many marketing messages we see in a day: http://www.hhcc.com/blog/the-elusive-advertising-clutter/

35. McLuhan, Marshall, *Understanding Media: The Extensions of Man* (McGraw-Hill, 1964).

36. Rogers, E. M., *Diffusion of Innovations (5th edition).* (Free Press, 2003).

Chapter 8

37. "value." Merriam-Webster.com. Merriam-Webster, 2011. Web. 8 February 2014.

38. Robert B. Woodruff, "Customer value: The next source for competitive advantage," Journal of the Academy of Marketing Science Volume 25, Issue 2, pp 139–153.

39. "Liquid Paper—Bette Nesmith Graham (1922–1980)" http://inventors.about.com/od/lstartinventions/a/liquid_paper.htm

40. Houston, A. "Strategic Insight 9—Is the JSF good enough?" Australian Strategic Policy Institute, 18 August 2004.

41. Michael E. Porter and Mark Kramer, "Creating Shared Value: how to reinvent capitalism—and unleash a wave of innovation and growth," Harvard Business Review, January-February 2011.

42. "Maintenance!" *One Quarter of U.S. Consumers Far More Likely to Spread the Word About a Bad Experience than a Good One.* Web. 20 May. 2014.

43. "The Top 100 List View." *Best Global Brands 2013.* Web. 14 Mar. 2014. <http://www.interbrand.com/en/best-global-brands/2013/top-100-list-view.aspx>.

Chapter 9

44. Pink, Dan. "Metaphor Marketing." Fast Company 1 Apr. 1998. Print.

45. "Choice, Happiness and Spaghetti Sauce." Malcolm Gladwell: Choice, Happiness and Spaghetti Sauce. TED. Web. 14 Apr. 2014. <http://www.ted.com/talks/malcolm_gladwell_on_spaghetti_sauce?language=en>.

46. Salter, Chuck. "Failure Doesn't Suck." *FastCompany*. FastCompany, 1 May 2007. Web. 16 Apr. 2014. <http://www.fastcompany.com/59549/failure-doesnt-suck>.

47. "How Many Times Should You Try Before Succeeding—Infographic." *Funders and Founders*. 28 Nov. 2012. Web. 20 Apr. 2014. <http://fundersandfounders.com/how-many-times-should-you-try/>.

48. A great article by Andrew Chen reflecting on the Techcrunch Bump: "After the Techcrunch Bump: Life in the "Trough of Sorrow"" Andrewchen.co. Web. 27 May 2014. <http://andrewchen.co/2012/09/10/after-the-techcrunch-bump-life-in-the-trough-of-sorrow/>

49. "2013CF Crowdfunding Industry Reports." *Industry Report*. Web. 7 Mar. 2014. <http://research.crowdsourcing.org/2013cf-crowdfunding-industry-report>.

50. "Crowdfunding Seen Providing $65 Billion Boost to the Global Economy in 2014 (Infographic)." *Entrepreneur*. Web. 4 Apr. 2014.

51. "KICKSTARTER." *Creator Handbook—Kickstarter*. Web. 13 Mar. 2014. <http://www.kickstarter.com/help/school?ref=footer#setting_your_goal>.

52. Neumeier, Marty, *The Brand Gap: How to Bridge the Distance between Business Strategy and Design: A Whiteboard Overview* (New Riders, 2006).

Chapter 10

53. Arango, Tim, and David Carr. "Netflix's Move Onto the Web Stirs Rivalries." *The New York Times*. The New York Times, 24 Nov. 2010. Web. 17 May 2014. <http://www.nytimes.com/2010/11/25/business/25netflix.html?pagewanted=1&hp>.

54. Amazon's Corporate Overview for Investors. You can access it here: http://phx.corporate-ir.net/phoenix.zhtml?c=176060&p=irol-mediaKit

55. @FAKEGRIMLOCK, "Minimum Viable Personality." AVC. Web. 27 Mar. 2014. <http://avc.com/2011/09/minimum-viable-personality/>

56. Sharp, Byron, *How Brands Grow: What Marketers Don't Know* (Oxford UP, 2010).

57. Hsieh, Tony, *Delivering Happiness: A Path to Profits, Passion, and Purpose*, (Business Plus, 2010).

Chapter 11

58. Christensen, Clayton M., *The Innovator's Dilemma: When New Technologies Cause Great Firms to Fail* (Harvard Business School, 1997).

OFFICIAL SPONSORS

This book was made possible through the support of our gracious sponsors. Thank you Peter Briscoe, Randy Hunt and Debbie Wooldridge for your early belief in this project.

ERICSSON

Etsy

ttc
Innovations

ABOUT THE AUTHOR

JEREMIAH GARDNER

Jeremiah Gardner is an author, speaker, lean brand practitioner, and bull-dog lover. He helps startups, entrepreneurs and Fortune 500 organizations reframe the way they think about brand innovation, culture, and leadership. He is the author of *The Lean Brand*, the first book to apply lean principles to branding, is a sought after speaker, and advises entrepreneurs around the world. Jeremiah lives in San Diego, California with his wife Jessie and their bulldog, Sir Hamilton.

Reach him on Twitter @JeremiahGardner or at
http://jeremiahgardner.com.

@JEREMIAHGARDNER

with BRANT COOPER

Brant Cooper helps organizations big and small innovate. He is the co-author of the New York Times Bestseller, *The Lean Entrepreneur* and is a sought after speaker, advisor and mentor. Brant previously authored *The Entrepreneur's Guide to Customer Development*, the first purpose-written book to discuss Lean Startup and Customer Development concepts, earning a distribution of over 50k. He has worked with thousands of entrepreneurs across the globe.

Reach him on Twitter @BrantCooper or at
http://movestheneedle.com.

@BRANTCOOPER

Made in the USA
San Bernardino, CA
19 October 2018